ReKindling Me

ReKindling Me

The No-BS Guide to ENDING BURNOUT & Reclaiming Your Power

Liz Atherton

CONSCIOUS CARE PUBLISHING PTY LTD

REKINDLING ME
The No-BS Guide to Ending Burnout & Reclaiming Your Power

Copyright © 2025 by Liz Atherton. All rights reserved.

First Published 2025 by: Conscious Care Publishing Pty Ltd
www.consciouscarepublishing.com

First Edition printed November 2025.

Notice of Rights:
This book is sold subject to the condition that it shall not, by way of trade or otherwise, be lent, resold, hired out, or otherwise circulated without the publisher's prior consent, in any form of binding or cover, other than that in which it is published, and without a similar condition, including this condition being imposed on the subsequent purchaser. All rights reserved by the publisher. No part of this publication may be reproduced, stored in a retrieval system, or transmitted in any form, or by any means, electronic, digital, mechanical, photocopying, scanning, recorded or otherwise, without the prior written permission of the copyright owner. Requests to the copyright owner should be addressed to Permissions Department, Conscious Care Publishing Pty Ltd, PO Box 2399, Redcliffe North, QLD 4020, Australia, email: admin@consciouscare.com

Limits of Liability/Disclaimer of Warranty:
While the publisher and author have used their best efforts in preparing this book, they make no representations or warranties with respect to the accuracy or completeness of the contents of this book and specifically disclaim any implied warranties of merchantability or fitness for a particular purpose. No warranty may be created or extended by sales representatives or written sales materials. The advice and strategies contained herein may not be suitable for your situation. You should consult with a professional where appropriate. The intent of the author is only to offer information for a general nature. Neither the publisher nor author shall be liable for any loss of profit or any other commercial damages, including but not limited to special, incidental, consequential, or other damages. The author and the publisher assume no responsibility for your actions.

Where photographic images have been provided by the author and people are depicted, such images are being used for illustrative purposes only. Product names may be trademarks or registered trademarks, and are used for identification and explanation without intent to infringe. Conscious Care Publishing publishes in a variety of print and electronic format and by print-on-demand. Some material included with standard print versions of this book may not be included in e-books or in print-on-demand. If this book refers to media such as a downloadable, CD or DVD that is not included in the version you purchased, you may download this material at the website nominated in the "Next Steps" section of this book.

National Library of Australia Cataloguing-in-Publication entry:
Author: Atherton, Liz
Rekindling Me / By Liz Atherton

ISBN 9780645089288 (Paperback)
ISBN 9780645089295 (ePub)
ISBN 9780987633729 (Workbook)
ISBN 9780987633736 (Audiobook)
ISBN 9781764210409 (Hardback)

Printed by Lightning Source
Typeset & cover design by Conscious Care Publishing Pty Ltd

ISBN: 978-0-6450892-8-8

For the ones who've held it all together for everyone else,
the ones who smile on the outside while quietly wondering,
"Why do I keep doing this?"

You're not broken.
You've just been brilliantly wired for survival.

This book is your permission slip to stop coping and
start coming home to yourself.

If you've been thinking there has to be more than this,
you were right.
There is.
And it starts here.

CONTENTS

ACKNOWLEDGMENTS	I
INTRODUCTION	III
AUTHOR'S NOTE	V

PART I

CHAPTER 1 - THE EXHAUSTION OF BEING THE STRONG ONE — 3
    Why You Became The Strong One — 5
    The Identity Trap — 7

CHAPTER 2 - BORN TO BELONG, TAUGHT TO TRADE: THE HIDDEN CURRENCY OF CHILDHOOD — 10
    The Human Currency: Trading — 11
    Conscious Trading — 13

CHAPTER 3 - YOU'RE NOT BROKEN – YOU'RE RUNNING OUTDATED SOFTWARE — 16
    Realigning with Your Core Self Beyond Trauma and Conditioning — 16
    Your Experience of Life Evolves as You Do — 17
    Misaligned Truths and the Challenge of Authentic Living — 18
    The Generational Nature of Programming — 19
    You Can't Heal by Fixing Others — 20
    The Cost of Conforming: When Survival Becomes Suppression — 21
    When Fear Becomes a Weapon — 21
    The Empath's Dilemma — 22
    Unconditional vs. Conditional Love — 22
    What Is Trauma? — 23

Your Brain's Role in Trauma	24
Unresolved Trauma and the Cycle of Pain	25

CHAPTER 4 - THE ARCHITECTURE OF STRESS: UNDERSTANDING THE INNER VOICES OF THE MIND — 27

Introduction: Where Stress Comes From	27
The Three Layers of The Mind: Freud's Classic Model	29
The Absence of the Adult Self Voice in Traumatised Areas	30
Jung's Contribution: The Shadow and the Collective Unconscious	31
Inner Voices in Dialogue: How Stress Manifests	31
How Trauma Silences the Adult Self	32
Realignment: Rebuilding The Internal Adult Self	33
The Psychic Apparatus (Id, Ego, Superego) In Communication	34
How Each Level Influences the Words You Choose, Your Tone, Your Body Language	34
The Gift of the Higher Self in Communication	39
Inner Voice Map for Conscious Conversations - Spotting the Voice in Conversations	41
Inviting The Higher Self to Lead Your Voice	42

CHAPTER 5 - STRESS ISN'T THE PROBLEM – IT'S THE MESSAGE — 46

The Emotional Battle Beneath the Surface	47
Two Emotional Languages: Natural And Distorted	48
Stress As a Symptom of Emotional Misalignment	50
The Vulnerability of Childhood Programming	50
The Subconscious Scripts You Inherited	51
Stress And the Survival Brain	52
Authenticity Is the Antidote	53
Rewiring The Subconscious	54
When Justified Emotions Are Still Misaligned	54
Layering Emotion to Stay Safe	56
When Coping Becomes Numbing	56
Why Thinking Alone Can't Heal You	57

The Real Work of Emotional Healing   58
When The Mind Can No Longer Hold the Pain   58
Healing Comes Through Recognition   59

PART II

CHAPTER 6 - HOW YOUR NERVOUS SYSTEM SHAPES YOUR INNER DIALOGUE   65

Your Body Is the First to Speak   66
The Mind-Body Connection: One Integrated System   67
How To Know What State You're In (Polyvagal Cues List)   68
Inner Dialogue - How the Body Shapes What You Tell Yourself   70
How Safety or Survival Shapes What You Say   71
Distorted Emotions = Distorted Communication   73
Words, Tone, And Pace - The Body's Tells   74
Calming Your System to Hear Your Soul   75
Clearing Survival Patterns: Tools For Rewiring the Body and Mind   78
Speaking From a Regulated State   81
Neuroscience-Based Change: The Fastest Path to Rewiring Survival Patterns   82
Simple Pre-Conversation Practices to Regulate Your System   84

CHAPTER 7 - DECODING EMOTIONAL TRIGGERS: PATHWAYS TO HEALING   91

What Are Triggers - And Why Do They Hijack Us?   92
How Triggers are Formed: The Emotional Blueprint of the Past   92
When the Past Hijacks the Present: How Triggers Distort Conversations   93
Rewiring Triggers: Freeing Your Voice for Authentic Expression 94

PART III

CHAPTER 8 - WHEN THE PAST SPEAKS THROUGH YOU: WHY OLD PROGRAMS DISTORT VOICE, TONE, AND PRESENCE   103

Why This Matters for Leadership and Life   106

Embodied Beliefs: Why Your Voice Reveals What You Believe	107

CHAPTER 9 - WHY MINDSET ALONE CAN'T CLEAR TRIGGERS — 111

When The Inner Child Overrides the Inner Parent	114
When The Inner Parent Silences or Controls the Inner Child	116
"I Know Better – But I Still React"	119
Your Survival Reflex - The Subconscious Mind, Nervous System, and Emotional Memory	120
How To Catch a Trigger in Mid-Flight	123
When Avoiding Pain Creates More of It	125
Why Talk Therapy Alone Isn't Enough	128
Why The Subconscious Isn't Reached Through Logic Alone	129
Mindset Doesn't Rewire - Experience Does	131
From Triggered to True: Why This Work Changes Everything	131
Why SCIENCE AND Soul Create Lasting Change	132

CHAPTER 10 - WHAT REWIRES THESE PATTERNS – SCIENCE + SOUL — 135

This Isn't Just Belief Change - It's Identity Restoration	139
This Is the Work We Do Inside the Rewrite & Ignite™ Program	140

CHAPTER 11 - BUILDING EMOTIONAL SAFETY WITHIN — 142

External vs Internal Safety	142
The Voices That Undermine Safety	143
Practices That Build Inner Safety (Foundational Habits)	143
Adult Self-Reassurance as a Nervous System Regulator	144
Reparenting as a Safety Practice	144
Rebuilding Trust with Yourself	144
Why Emotional Safety is the Foundation of Authentic Voice	145

PART IV

CHAPTER 12 - THE LANGUAGE OF THE HIGHER SELF — 149

How To Recognise the Higher Self in Real Time	151
How The Higher Self Speaks in Everyday Life	152

Why The Higher Self Isn't Always Loud	153
Practising Listening to Higher Self Speech	154
How To Strengthen the Connection	156
Why This Matters in Communication, Leadership & Life	156

CHAPTER 13 - CONSCIOUS BOUNDARIES AND SOUL INTEGRITY — 160

The Nervous System and Boundaries	162
The Voices Behind Weak or Rigid Boundaries	163
Boundaries Are Not Walls - They Are Bridges	166
Soul Integrity: Living Aligned with What You Know	167
When Boundaries Are Resisted or Misunderstood	169
Higher Self Boundary Scripts	170
What It Sounds Like When Your Boundaries Are Met with Resistance, Misunderstanding, Guilt or Even Anger	171

PART V

CHAPTER 14 - RECLAIMING YOUR AUTHENTIC VOICE — 179

Why Your Voice was Hidden (And Why That's Not Your Fault)	179
Your Voice as Leadership	181

CHAPTER 15 - INTEGRATING THE ARCHITECTURE: LIVING THE SHIFT — 184

The Collapse Before Resurrection	185
Living From Soul Integrity	187
From Healing to Leading	187
The Journey Is Ongoing - But You're Equipped	188
What Soul Integrity Looks Like in Real Life	190
Final Alignment Practice: Your Soul-Led Contract	191

CHAPTER 16 - YOUR PATH FORWARD FROM HERE — 195

Helping to Heal Others	195

NEXT STEPS... — 199

Disclaimer:

The practices, perspectives, and tools in this book are offered for educational and personal development purposes only. They are not intended as a substitute for psychological, medical, or psychiatric treatment or professional advice.

While I have over 25 years of experience as a life coach, intuitive guide, and spiritual mentor, I am not a licensed psychologist, therapist, or medical professional. The guidance within this book is drawn from client work, intuitive insight, my own healing journey, and teachings received through spirit and Higher Self connection.

Every reader is responsible for how they engage with and apply the material in this book. If you are experiencing significant emotional distress or mental health challenges, please seek the support of a qualified professional.

This book is not meant to diagnose, treat, or cure any condition. What you choose to do with the information here is entirely your responsibility, and your healing journey is sacred, personal, and always your own.

ACKNOWLEDGMENTS

To my mini-me, my daughter Katie. Your fierce determination and fearless pursuit of your dreams inspire me every day. You came into this world to teach me more about myself than I ever could have imagined. Your light and love shines brightly, touching so many with your kindness, compassion, and support, while standing strong in your boundaries and inner wisdom. You are the embodiment of strength with heart. My world changed in incredible ways when you came into it.

To my son Lachlan, your quiet strength and unwavering resolve light the path of your life in a way that commands admiration. You live with honour, resilience, and independence. You are proof that pain can be alchemised into purpose, and your soul has gifted me the deepest lessons in love and protection. Though you are my son, you carry the rare qualities of a true leader, protector, and provider.

I am, without a doubt, the proudest mum on earth and I've grown immeasurably because you both chose me.

To my beautiful grandchildren. You are pure joy. Your presence reminds me daily of what truly matters, and your innocence and laughter keep my spirit young.

To my dear Auntie May. Thank you for stepping in with unconditional love and grace when I needed a mother most. Though you've now earned your wings, your kindness lives on, etched in my heart.

To my cheerful Grandfather Walter Christie. Your unwavering devotion to family, your wisdom, and your legacy of love continue to guide and ground me. I still feel your presence often. Steady, proud, and smiling.

And to my beloved Mum and Dad. Though you left this world far too soon, your love never left me. You continue to walk beside me in spirit, reminding me of where I came from, and nudging me forward into the woman I've become. The passion and purpose I live today is part of the gift you planted in me.

With all my love and deepest gratitude to you all.

INTRODUCTION

After more than 25 years of working closely with clients navigating life's challenges, trauma, and inner conflict, I felt called to write this book, a gentle companion for those seeking to find themselves again amidst the chaos of life, family, finances, and relationships, and to lead their lives on their terms.

From the moment we're born, life begins shaping us. Some of us are nurtured. Some are neglected, hurt, or pushed to grow too fast. Whether we start our lives with abundance or adversity, our journey is uniquely our own. That journey, layered with inherited beliefs, generational patterns, societal expectations, and the tension between nature and nurture, begins to define who we think we are.

We all arrive as innocent, pristine beings, perfect, like uncut diamonds. But over time, the weight of our experiences can leave us feeling like we're nothing more than a lump of carbon. The truth is: we are still diamonds, buried beneath the layers of outdated beliefs, emotional scars, and unconscious programming.

This book is about **reclaiming your brilliance**. It's about reconnecting with your true self, your soul essence, your intuitive knowing, your inner freedom. It's about healing from the beliefs and emotional patterns that no longer serve you and awakening the life you were meant to live: one of purpose, joy, clarity, and wholeness.

Whether you're feeling lost, anxious, stuck, or simply tired of the internal battles, know this: **you can change your life**. When you begin to understand how your mind works, how old voices from the past still whisper in the present, you can reclaim your power. You can calm the inner chatter, release distorted emotions, and stop living life on autopilot.

You were never broken. You were only conditioned. And that conditioning can be healed.

This is your invitation to rediscover who you truly are beneath the noise. It's time to rekindle the real you.

With love and purpose,

AUTHOR'S NOTE

Like many of you, I've lived through life's highs and lows. Its joys, heartbreaks, emotional twists, and hard-earned awakenings. I've walked the path of inner conflict, questioning, healing, and eventually transformation. Through it all, I've come to understand that the mind is not our enemy, it's misunderstood. When we learn how it operates and why we hold onto pain, we unlock the keys to freedom.

After writing *Mind Chatter That Matters*, I deepened my understanding of how our limiting beliefs and stored emotional pain, often born from childhood or trauma, can be healed. But I also discovered that when our beliefs conflict with our inner values, a powerful inner war begins. Without resolution, this conflict quietly shapes our lives and can hold us back for decades.

As a life coach and psychic medium, I've had the privilege of blending spiritual insight with science-backed modalities, particularly neuroscience, to help others reprogram their minds and reconnect with their true selves. I've channelled messages from spirit, received wisdom beyond logic, and guided many through their transformation. But my journey didn't begin in a textbook or a healing room, it started in childhood.

I was introduced to spirituality by my father, who had a near-death experience before I was born. After he passed when I was just 24, his presence remained a guiding force in my life. Then, at 32, I lost my beautiful mother. Her passing fractured the family, as often happens when the matriarchal figure transitions. Different beliefs and unhealed wounds surfaced, and we disbanded in our grief.

My spiritual awakening began at the age of eight. Even as a child, I felt like I was in a movie, everyone else playing a role in *my* experience. I used to wonder why I had been placed in a family with so many challenges. Today, I know I chose that soul contract. I was born into this family to grow, to awaken, and to find my path; one of purpose, passion, and service.

Losing both parents at a young age was a spiritual catalyst, but it left me aching. I needed their arms around me. I needed their guidance, their ongoing love, support and belief in me. But the universe had other plans. At the time of my mother's passing, I had a young daughter, nearly four, who became my first living miracle and gave me the strength to carry on. Three years later, I was blessed with a son. Doctors had told me I couldn't conceive after a ruptured ectopic pregnancy, but Spirit had different intentions.

For most of their lives, I was a single mother, raising two children, running a business, and living on acreage with no family support. I was it. I've faced the dark corridors of life: the pain of losing an unborn child, sexual abuse, financial ruin, divorce, loss of loved ones, domestic violence; physical, emotional, and financial, both in childhood and adulthood. I've known emptiness. But from that emptiness, I grew strong. From the ruins, I built resilience.

Experiences shape us, but only if we allow them to define us. Healing means learning to reframe the past, so we can release it and return to the authentic self that lives beneath all the noise. The *real* you. The *free* you. The reason your soul chose this earthly plane.

Earth is not an easy classroom for souls. But it is rich with opportunity. We choose our family. We choose our challenges. As part of this journey, we even decide to forget who we are, so we can remember again. This journey is not about suffering. It's about returning and coming home to self.

I hope this book helps you find that home within. May it bring clarity where there has been confusion, peace where there has been pain, and the healing your heart has been quietly asking for.

With love and light,

Part I

Wired to Survive, Born to Be Free

Why your voice was never the problem — it was your programming.

Much of what drives your reactions, your communication, and your stress was formed long before you were old enough to question it. As children we learn how to belong. We learn what earns love. We learn what keeps us safe. Over time those lessons become patterns. Patterns that shape how you relate to others, how you handle pressure, and how you see yourself in the world. These patterns are not flaws. They were survival strategies. But what once helped you survive may now be quietly limiting how freely you live. In this section we begin uncovering those patterns. Because when you can see the pattern, you are no longer trapped inside it.

1

THE EXHAUSTION OF BEING THE STRONG ONE

The exhaustion of being the strong one rarely comes from what you do. It comes from how long you have been carrying it alone. If you are used to being the strong one, people rarely ask how you are. They assume you are fine. You are the one who handles things. The one who figures it out. The one who steadies the room when everything else feels chaotic.

People rely on you because you are capable. They lean on you because you are dependable. And over time, that becomes your role. You carry the emotional weight.

You solve the problems. You keep things moving when others shut down. From the outside, it looks like strength. From the inside, it can feel like quiet exhaustion. Not the kind of tired that comes from a busy week. The kind that builds over years of being the one who absorbs the impact for everyone else.

Most people do not see how much you carry. They simply expect you to keep carrying it. And the truth is, you do not want sympathy. You do not want applause. You want something far simpler and far more human. You want someone to look at you and say, *"Put it down. I've got this."* And for a moment, you want to believe that you can.

I know this pattern well. I have lived inside it myself. I know it intimately. I lived as the strong one for a long time. And the truth is, most people do not see how much you carry.

And this is something many strong people never realise. The role you learned to play was not your true identity. It was programming. Programming shaped by the environments you grew up in, the expectations placed on you, and the ways you learned to stay connected to others. What once helped you survive slowly became the way you lived. And over time, that role became so familiar you stopped questioning it.

Many people who live as the strong one do not realise how much of their life has been shaped by that role. It rarely begins as a conscious choice. It grows quietly over time. You become the one who holds things together because someone has to. When situations become unstable, you are the one who steps forward. When emotions rise in a room, you are the one who absorbs them. When others feel overwhelmed, you steady the ground beneath them.

People start to depend on that. They call you when they need advice. They come to you when something breaks. They lean on you because you seem capable of handling what others cannot. And at first, that can feel meaningful. Being dependable brings a sense of purpose. It can feel good to be the one people trust. But there is another side to it.

When you are always the strong one, you are rarely the one who gets held. When you are the capable one, people assume you do not need support. When you are the one who steadies everyone else, few people stop to ask what steadies you.

And after a while, something subtle begins to happen. People stop seeing your strength as effort. They begin to see it as who you are. So they depend on it. And slowly, without anyone intending it, you become the person who carries more than anyone realises.

Over time, strength stops being something you use when needed. It becomes something you perform all the time. And that is where exhaustion begins.

Underneath your "Strong One" identity, there is often an invisible agreement. It is rarely spoken out loud, let alone acknowledged, yet it quietly governs how you move through life. The agreement sounds something like this.

- I will hold it together.
- I will absorb the impact.
- I will manage the emotions.
- I will solve the problems.
- I will not collapse.

On the outside, you may look calm, functional, and reliable. People trust you. They expect things from you. Sometimes they even criticise you when you do not meet their expectations.

But what they do not necessarily see is how much responsibility you quietly carry. The deeper wound in this pattern is not simply the workload. It is the unspoken fear that if you stop carrying everything, people might stop choosing you. If you stop being useful, will you still be valued? If you stop being dependable, will people still stay?

Many people who live as the strong one carry this fear without even realising it. Their value has become linked to their usefulness, and that is a heavy identity to maintain.

WHY YOU BECAME THE STRONG ONE

No one wakes up one day and decides to become hyper independent.

You became capable because life trained you to be.

You learned to rely on yourself because there were times when no one else stepped in. You learned to steady the emotional atmosphere because someone needed to. You learned to solve problems because problems still had to be solved.

When you were not protected, you became the protector. When you were not consistently seen, you became the achiever. When you were not chosen in the ways you needed to be, you learned to become indispensable. Strength began as a survival skill.

At first, it was simply a way to navigate difficult circumstances, a way to make sure life kept moving forward. But somewhere along the way, the skill slowly became identity. Instead of using strength when it was needed, you started living inside it. And when strength becomes identity, rest becomes difficult, if not impossible.

Burnout does not always look like collapse. Sometimes it looks like control. Sometimes it looks like distance. Sometimes it looks like being the most capable person in the room. Depending on how you learned to survive, burnout can show up in different ways.

Some people respond to pressure by doing more. You take responsibility for everything. You feel uneasy when others are unreliable, so you step in before anyone even asks. You organise, fix, manage, and achieve because experience has taught you that if you do not handle it, things might fall apart. But beneath that capability sits a quiet exhaustion.

You feel frustrated when no one steps in for you. You struggle to relax when others appear careless or disorganised. You feel deeply hurt when your effort goes unnoticed. Even when you feel overwhelmed, you keep pushing. You have learned that everything depends on you.

For others, burnout hides behind independence. You pride yourself on not needing anyone. You value competence, logic, and self-sufficiency. When situations become emotionally intense, you pull back rather than lean in. You work harder instead of talking about feelings. You shut down rather than arguing. Somewhere along the way, you may have decided that relying on people leads to disappointment. So, you handle things yourself. From the outside, you appear calm and composed. But underneath, you are carrying life alone.

Burnout does not always appear to be emotional. It can show up as numbness, irritation, or quiet withdrawal. Instead of reaching out for support, you convince yourself that independence is strength.

For others, some people move between closeness and distance, craving connection, yet also fear it. You can invest deeply in relationships and then suddenly withdraw when something feels unsafe. Criticism can feel devastating. Loyalty becomes something you test, even if you do not realise you are doing it. You want closeness, yet you also feel overwhelmed by it. This cycle can feel confusing and exhausting.

Although these responses look different on the surface, they often grow from the same root. At some point in life, connection did not feel safe. So, your nervous system built a strategy to protect you. The strategy worked. Until it began to cost you more energy than it gave back, or it no longer protects you and begins to sabotage you instead.

THE IDENTITY TRAP

Burnout is not only about how much you do. It is about who you believe you must be. When your identity becomes the strong one, the rational one, the fixer, the high performer, or the person who never needs anyone, there is no room left to rest. Strength becomes something you feel required to prove. But proving strength is exhausting.

The protector identity can feel powerful for a long time. It gives you control, purpose, and a sense of direction. Yet eventually it can become a prison. If you are always the strong one, you never get to be held. If you are always the capable one, you rarely get to feel supported. If you are always the leader, you never fully exhale. And over time, that pressure begins to wear down even the strongest people.

You do not have to stop being strong to reclaim your life. But you do need to stop proving it. True strength is not about carrying everything indefinitely. It is about knowing when something is yours to hold and when it is not. It is the ability to lead your life from a place of grounded self-trust, rather than constant responsibility. This is what sovereignty looks like.

You can still be capable without over carrying. You can still be dependable without absorbing every emotional impact around you. You can still lead without needing to control or fix everything. You can love people without earning your place in their lives. And you can rest without guilt. Burnout is not a sign that you are weak. It is often the signal that an old survival strategy has reached its limit.

You are not broken. You are patterned. And patterns can be rewritten. Not by pushing harder. But by learning to lead yourself differently.

The question most people begin asking at this point is simple. How did I become the strong one in the first place? To answer that, we need to go back to the very beginning of life. To the place where most of our patterns were first formed.

REFLECTION & INTEGRATION

Before we go deeper into how these patterns form, take a moment to look honestly at your own experience. You may recognise yourself in some of the patterns we just explored. See what resonates with you.

Ask yourself:

- Do I feel responsible for holding things together for others?
- Do people come to me when they need help, advice, or emotional support?
- Do I find it difficult to ask for help, or do I rarely even think to ask, even when I need it?

- Do I keep going when I am exhausted because others rely on me?
- Do I feel resentful when my efforts go unnoticed?
- Do I struggle to relax when things feel out of control around me?
- Do I often feel like the strong one in my family, relationships, or workplace?

If several of these resonate, you may have learned early in life that strength and usefulness were the safest ways to stay connected to others.

There is nothing wrong with being capable or dependable. But when strength becomes the only role you feel allowed to play, it can quietly disconnect you from your own needs.

Now ask yourself something deeper:

- Where did I first learn that I needed to be the strong one?
- Was it in my family?
- In my relationships?
- In moments where I felt I had no other choice?

Take a few minutes to write whatever comes to mind. There is no right or wrong answer here. The goal is simply awareness. Because once you begin to see the pattern, you are already one step closer to changing it.

2

BORN TO BELONG, TAUGHT TO TRADE: THE HIDDEN CURRENCY OF CHILDHOOD

Your value doesn't come from what you trade to be loved. It comes from remembering you were love before you ever had to earn it.

Even though we arrive in this world through our parents, we are ultimately here on our own soul's journey. Our parents may give us our physical form through genetics. Still, they also contribute much more, emotionally and mentally, through their nurturing (or lack thereof), their beliefs, and the life standards they model. Beyond them, we are further shaped by other caregivers, extended family, society, and cultural norms.

At times, it can feel like we are simply at the mercy of our birth circumstances: the family we were born into, the time and place, the generational patterns passed down, and the emotional maturity-or immaturity-of those raising us.

When you look at life through a wider lens, the irony becomes clear: human beings are capable of creating children long before they are capable of raising them with wisdom and understanding. Girls as young as nine begin the biological journey into motherhood. Yet, emotional maturity may not arrive until decades later, often not until a woman's thirties, or a man's forties. This means that, more often than not, children are raised by other children in adult bodies. Individuals who have not yet resolved their inner wounds, beliefs, heartbreaks, and conditioning.

There's truth in the saying: **"Hurt people hurt people."** If your caregivers never had the opportunity, tools, or awareness to heal their own pain, they are likely to pass that pain along, unintentionally, but powerfully. So, who is to blame?

Can we fault our parents for doing the best they could with what they knew at the time? Can we point the finger at others while repeating the very same patterns ourselves, unaware, unhealed, and projecting? The honest answer is **NO**.

Blame keeps you stuck. It creates a revolving door of suffering that strips you of your power and delays your healing. Taking responsibility for your healing doesn't mean excusing the actions of others. It means reclaiming your ability to move forward.

THE HUMAN CURRENCY: TRADING

We live in a world built on trade. We trade for goods, for money, for time, experiences, status, even for love. From our earliest days, we begin to trade parts of ourselves; our time, energy, self-worth, happiness, even our authenticity, to receive love, belonging, safety, validation, and approval.

We are conditioned to trade. It's built into our social fabric. And most of us aren't even aware we're doing it.

From a young age, even nurturing becomes transactional. Caregivers often give love or approval in exchange for certain behaviours and withdraw it when we don't comply. This becomes the foundation of our understanding of love: **conditional and earned.**

Whether consciously or unconsciously, most people continue this pattern throughout life. And although many trades seem benign, *"I'll help you if you help me"*, what lies beneath is often a form of masked manipulation. When someone gives love, attention, or support not freely, but to gain something in return, it becomes a **conditional exchange** rather than a genuine expression of love and affection.

Trading often hides in the guise of love, but at its core, it's a transaction: one person giving up something, so another doesn't have to. Whether out of laziness, fear, entitlement, or insecurity, it creates dependency. Love becomes something to earn, not something freely given or received.

As children, we have no choice but to trade to survive. We rely on others for food, shelter, love, and safety. And in doing so, we learn that **compliance earns connection,** or at the very least, reduces rejection. This pattern is reinforced not just in families but through culture, school, religion, and media. Even the most well-meaning parents and conscious caregivers can unintentionally reinforce this cycle.

However, here's the truth: trading, when done **unconsciously,** leads to emotional exhaustion and spiritual **disconnection.**

You begin to give more than you genuinely want to give. You silence yourself. You shrink. You comply, not from love, but from fear of losing love. And when the trade becomes imbalanced, when expectations are not met or reciprocated, you may feel resentful, used, or even abused.

This is the emotional cost of unconscious trading.

You may give out of fear of abandonment. You may rebel and then feel rejected. You may keep giving, hoping someone will notice. But all the while, you're trading pieces of yourself; your truth, your energy, your joy. To be seen, heard, and accepted.

CONSCIOUS TRADING

To stop living in the loop of unconscious trading is to wake up. To see clearly how families, systems, and societies have conditioned us. It is the beginning of liberation.

When you trade consciously, you begin to choose when, why, how, and with whom you give or receive. You reclaim the power to decide rather than react. You can still give, but from a place of alignment, not obligation.

You no longer need to give away your soul just to be loved.

This doesn't mean you stop giving. It means you stop giving yourself away.

You no longer trade your boundaries for approval.

You no longer trade your peace for someone else's comfort.

You no longer shape-shift just to be accepted.

You no longer trade your self-worth for someone else's approval.

You no longer shape-shift your truth for connection.

Instead, you begin to live from your truth, a place of sovereignty. You give from overflow, not depletion. You engage from awareness, not fear. You offer yourself, not to be chosen, but because you've chosen you first. You align with your Higher Self. And from that place, you select your exchanges, freely, joyfully, and without attachment.

This is the path to living as your authentic self. No more surviving by compliance. No more bartering your joy. Just you, whole, sovereign, and empowered. A life where you no longer need to trade to survive, but choose to engage, connect, and give from freedom. And from that space, everything changes.

That is the beginning of returning to your true self.

~

You can download a workbook to help you complete all of the *Reflections & Integration* sections of this book. You can download this workbook at lizatherton.com/rkm-workbook.

REFLECTION & INTEGRATION

Reflection Prompt

Take a quiet moment to reflect on this question:

- Where in my life am I trading my time, energy, truth, or peace in exchange for love, approval, or safety?

Now ask yourself the deeper question:

- What am I most afraid to lose, and how often do I abandon myself to keep it?

There is no need for shame. This is simply about awareness. Naming the trade is the first act of reclaiming your power.

Simple Exercise

For the next 3 days, choose one interaction per day; at work, in family, in friendship or partnership, and reflect:

- What did I give?
- What did I hope to receive in return?
- Was this trade aligned with my truth, or driven by fear?
- If I had traded consciously, what would I have done differently?

Write it down. Don't edit yourself. Let the truth rise.

By the end of the three days, look at your notes and ask:
- What patterns do I see?
- What's one trade am I ready to stop making?

That one choice could be the beginning of returning to your true self.

3

YOU'RE NOT BROKEN – YOU'RE RUNNING OUTDATED SOFTWARE

You were never broken. You were brilliantly adaptive in a world that didn't always honour your light. But now, you are free to remember who you truly are.

REALIGNING WITH YOUR CORE SELF BEYOND TRAUMA AND CONDITIONING

The point of human life is not perfection or constant happiness. It's to remember who we are, not just from a place of spiritual knowing, but through the tangible, often messy, physical experience of living. We enter this world as pure, connected beings, full of potential and light. But we also enter into density, into the heaviness of human life with all its complexities, emotions, expectations, and constructs.

And through this density, we forget.

We forget our spiritual identity. We forget the feeling of being safe and whole within ourselves. We often forget how it feels to live by our truth.

But this forgetting is not a mistake. It's part of the sacred journey. In forgetting, we begin to seek. And in seeking, we begin to remember, not just intellectually, but through every experience that challenges, stretches, and transforms us. This is how the world evolves. By us forgetting our true nature so we can rediscover it through growth, choice, and healing.

What changes most throughout life is not just what happens to us, but how we relate to it. Our relationship with our experiences, the meanings we give them, the beliefs we form, and the energy we carry around them, that's what shapes our reality. Your life is an ever-evolving reflection of your inner world. The more you align with your core self, the more your outer world begins to reflect that truth.

As spiritual beings having a human experience, we expand creation itself by engaging in the process of forgetting and remembering. We agree to enter the physical world with limited awareness, to experience pain, joy, confusion, love, and contrast. This isn't a punishment. It's a divine agreement to evolve, to contribute to the ongoing growth of consciousness through our personal transformation.

YOUR EXPERIENCE OF LIFE EVOLVES AS YOU DO

At different stages of life, our perceptions change. What once felt impossible becomes manageable. What felt like our truth is revealed as conditioning. With age, if we allow it, comes wisdom, the kind of wisdom born not from theory, but from lived experience. Often, it's only after years of feeling disconnected, misaligned, or overwhelmed that we begin to return to our essence. It's not uncommon for people to feel more themselves in their 40s or 50s than they ever did in their 20s.

This isn't failure. This is awakening.

In our earlier years, we may live in ways that don't align with our inner truth, pursuing things that don't fulfill us, maintaining relationships that drain us, or adopting roles that were never meant for us in the first place. It's only later, often after loss or crisis, that we realise how far we've drifted from ourselves. But this realisation is powerful. It signals the beginning of a return, a reconnection to what has always been within us.

This book is an invitation to accelerate that return. To look closely at the internal programming that has been running your life, programming built from early beliefs, past traumas, and unconscious patterns. Most of these programs were never consciously chosen. They were inherited, absorbed, or adopted for the sake of survival.

But survival is not the same as living.

This journey is about letting go of what no longer serves your growth and returning to alignment with your essence; your soul, your spirit, your truth. When you do, you naturally begin to live with more joy, clarity, peace, and purpose.

MISALIGNED TRUTHS AND THE CHALLENGE OF AUTHENTIC LIVING

How can we live authentically when the foundation of our thoughts, emotions, and behaviours is built on experiences that often taught us the opposite?

It's no wonder we struggle to feel whole. We're trying to build a life of joy, freedom, and authenticity on top of subconscious programming that says:

- *"You're only lovable if you're perfect."*
- *"Your needs don't matter."*
- *"You must please others to be safe."*
- *"You're too much."*

- *"You're not enough."*

These beliefs didn't come from your soul. They came from your early experiences, many of which were outside your control. When we are young, we can't yet discern what's true or not. We absorb everything, spoken and unspoken, as truth. Our survival depends on our caregivers, and so we conform to their expectations, fears, and limitations, even if it means denying our own truth.

Living authentically requires that we examine these beliefs. We must ask: *Do these beliefs reflect who I am now? Or are they echoes of someone else's pain?*

Reclaiming your authenticity isn't about rebellion, it's about realignment. It's about letting go of the programming that was built to keep you safe in the past but limits your growth in the present.

THE GENERATIONAL NATURE OF PROGRAMMING

Our parents and caregivers were shaped by their own programming, influenced by their experiences and upbringing. Often, they passed on beliefs and behaviours they never had the chance to question or heal. Most of them didn't wake up each day thinking, *"How can I damage my child's sense of self today?"* They were simply doing what they knew, often unconsciously repeating patterns that were passed down to them.

When we begin to awaken, it's easy to fall into the trap of blame. We might think, *"If only my parents had been more loving, more present, more conscious, I'd be okay."* But this mindset keeps us tethered to the pain. It places our power outside ourselves.

Healing begins when we stop pointing fingers and start looking inward, not to blame ourselves, but to take responsibility for our own healing. We must accept that while we didn't choose the original pain, we now have the power to decide how we respond to it.

Blame keeps us stuck. Responsibility sets us free.

When you understand that your belief systems were created because of unprocessed experiences, you gain the power to change them. This doesn't mean excusing harmful behaviour, it means choosing not to let it define you. It means saying, *"This pattern may have started before me, but it ends with me."*

YOU CAN'T HEAL BY FIXING OTHERS

One of the most painful realisations on the healing journey is this: **you cannot change someone else to heal yourself.** No matter how much you want your parents, your partner, or your friends to understand, validate, or love you differently, your healing can't depend on their transformation.

If the people who raised you never found their way back to their true selves, they may never be able to give you what you needed. And that's devastating. But it's also freeing. Because once you stop waiting for someone else to change, you can begin the work of meeting your own needs; of becoming the parent, the protector, the nurturer, and the guide you always needed.

When we are born, our survival depends on others. We rely on our caregivers for love, nurturing, and protection. This need is biological. But as we grow, many of us never update this belief. We continue to seek externally what must be found internally.

We forget that we *are* love. That our soul's essence is love, peace, and worthiness. However, because we are conditioned to seek love outside of ourselves, we become disconnected from it. And in that disconnection, the suffering begins.

THE COST OF CONFORMING: WHEN SURVIVAL BECOMES SUPPRESSION

*You are not required to set yourself
on fire to keep others warm.*

In early life, we conform out of necessity. We shape ourselves into what our caregivers want or need, because we cannot survive without their approval or support. We become quiet when we want to speak. We act "good" even when we feel angry or afraid. We make ourselves small so others feel more **comfortable.**

But over time, this compliance becomes suppression. The more we ignore our truth in pursuit of safety or love, the more we lose sight of our authentic selves. We begin to identify with the role we play, rather than the soul we are.

And that's when suffering begins.

Because no matter how good you are at pleasing others, deep down, your soul will ache for something real. You'll feel the dissonance between who you pretend to be and who you really are. That ache isn't something to fix, it's something to listen to. It's your inner being calling you back home.

WHEN FEAR BECOMES A WEAPON

Fear is one of the most powerful tools of control, and it often begins in childhood. We're taught to fear disapproval, rejection, and abandonment. We learn that speaking our truth could mean punishment or withdrawal of love. These early fears persist into adulthood, shaping how we relate to others and ourselves.

Often, others will use fear to influence you, not always maliciously, but because they, too, were taught to survive by manipulating or controlling others. They may say things like:

- *"If you loved me, you'd do this for me."*
- *"You'll regret it if you leave."*

- *"You're selfish for putting yourself first."*

These statements are often rooted in their own insecurity and need to feel safe. However, when we are unaware of these dynamics, we internalise them and begin to sacrifice our needs, dreams, and desires to avoid conflict or loss.

Becoming conscious means recognising these patterns and reclaiming your power. It means pausing before reacting and asking yourself, *"Is this fear mine, or has it been projected onto me?"*

THE EMPATH'S DILEMMA

For those who are highly sensitive or empathic, this dynamic can be even more pronounced. You may feel others' emotions so deeply that you confuse them with your own. You may over-give, over-care, over-perform, just to keep others from feeling pain or discomfort.

But this often leads to emotional burnout, resentment, and self-abandonment. You begin to feel used, taken for granted, or betrayed, yet it's your pattern of overextending that made those dynamics possible.

This isn't about blame. It's about awareness.

When you give out of obligation or fear, you're not giving from love, you're giving from survival. The most healing shift you can make is to offer from a place of fullness, not emptiness. To give when you *choose*, not when you feel you *must*. This is how self-honouring begins to grow.

UNCONDITIONAL VS. CONDITIONAL LOVE

One of the most foundational aspects of healing is understanding the kind of love you received, and the kind you now seek.

Conditional Love

This is the love most of us were taught to accept. It's a transaction, even if unspoken: *"If you behave, I will love you. If you please me, I will stay. If you make me proud, I will give you approval."* It is love given with strings, measured by performance, and often withdrawn when expectations aren't met.

This kind of love teaches us that we must earn our worth. It teaches us to conform, to suppress, and to monitor whether we are "enough constantly." The fear of disappointing others becomes our compass.

Unconditional Love

Unconditional love is rare, but it is real. It is love without demand, without control, without condition. It is not passive or boundary-less, but it does not require you to be anyone other than who you truly are.

True spiritual love says, *"I see you, and I accept you fully, even when you are messy, confused, or imperfect."*

When we begin to offer ourselves this kind of love, we stop chasing it from others. We stop negotiating for approval. We stop apologising for existing.

We remember that love isn't something we earn, it's something we are.

When we internalise either conditional or unconditional love, it becomes our inner dialogue on how we treat ourselves and others.

WHAT IS TRAUMA?

Trauma is not only about catastrophic events. It's about what overwhelms your ability to cope in the moment, especially without support. It's emotional or energetic fragmentation, when you feel alone, unsafe, or helpless and lack the resources to process what's happening.

Trauma is stored in your nervous system and subconscious mind. It stays locked away because, at the time, it was too much to face. The mind, in its brilliance, stores it away so you can continue surviving. But eventually, those stored experiences leak into your adult life. They shape your triggers, fears, beliefs, and emotional reactions.

Two people can go through the same event, but one experiences trauma while the other does not. Why? Trauma is less about the event and more about whether the person felt supported, safe, and resourced at the time.

You can experience trauma from:

- A parent yelling at you
- Being ignored when you needed comfort
- Feeling unwanted or unseen
- A sudden loss, change, or betrayal
- Neglect, abuse, assaults, conflict or the exposure of it
- Accidents
- Natural disasters
- Unexpected loss
- Witnessing violence.

The more often these things happen without resolution, the more your system internalises a state of threat.

YOUR BRAIN'S ROLE IN TRAUMA

Let's explore what's happening biologically when trauma occurs.

The Prefrontal Cortex (Your Rational Brain)

This part of the brain is responsible for decision-making, logic, problem-solving, and regulating emotion. However, it doesn't fully develop until your mid-20s. That means many early traumatic experiences aren't processed with reason. They're processed emotionally and subconsciously.

The Amygdala (Your Emotional Brain)

The amygdala acts like a threat detector. When something painful or frightening happens, it sounds the alarm and activates your survival response: fight, flight, freeze, or fawn.

When an emotion is too intense to process, the brain stores it, along with the associated belief, so that you can avoid similar pain in the future. This is why triggers feel so intense and sometimes irrational. Your emotional brain is reacting to a perceived threat based on a past event, even if your logical brain knows it's no longer dangerous.

If those emotions are never revisited, reframed, or healed, they remain frozen in time, affecting your adult responses long after the original event.

UNRESOLVED TRAUMA AND THE CYCLE OF PAIN

When trauma remains unresolved, it creates patterns that are often invisible until we begin to wake up. You may notice:

- Overreacting emotionally to certain situations
- Shutting down in conflict
- Feeling like a helpless child when challenged
- Struggling to trust or feel safe in relationships
- Seeking validation through over achievement or perfectionism.

These patterns are not flaws. Your system is doing what it was programmed to do to protect you.

However, now that you are an adult, you can update the system. You can bring awareness, healing, and compassion to the parts of you that were wounded. You can learn to regulate your nervous system, shift your beliefs, and build new patterns that reflect who you are, not who you had to become.

REFLECTION & INTEGRATION

Reflection Prompt

Where do I still trade parts of myself for love, safety, or approval?

What would it feel like to live from my core, without the fear of rejection?

Journal Exercise – Writing to Your Inner Child

Write a letter to the part of you that felt unsupported or abandoned.

Let them know you are here now and they are no longer alone. That their needs matter, their pain is valid, and they don't have to carry it anymore.

Offer them compassion, and begin to rebuild the bridge between your Adult Self and the Inner Child within.

Belief Rewriting Practice

List three outdated beliefs from childhood.

Then, for each one, write a new belief that reflects your truth today.

Example:

- **Old:** *"My needs are a burden."*
- **New:** *"My needs are valid and deserve to be met."*

4

THE ARCHITECTURE OF STRESS: UNDERSTANDING THE INNER VOICES OF THE MIND

Until you make the unconscious conscious, it will direct your life, and you will call it fate – Carl Jung.

You are not broken, you are layered. The words you speak, the tones you use, the reactions that rise from your chest…they are all shaped by the deeper architecture of your mind and heart.

The child within you speaks. The adult negotiates. The inner critic scolds. And deeper still, the voice of your soul whispers.

Learning to hear these voices, and choosing which one you allow to lead your communication, is how you begin to heal not only your relationships with others, but also your relationship with yourself.

INTRODUCTION: WHERE STRESS COMES FROM

We often believe that stress stems from external pressures in life, work, finances, relationships, or time management. While these are common triggers, they are not the actual source. The real origin of stress lies within the **architecture of the human mind**, in the inner conflict that arises when different parts of our psyche are in opposition to one another. The present situation doesn't cause most communication breakdowns, triggers, and emotional reactions in relationships, they are **echoes of unresolved inner dynamics**.

This inner conflict often operates beneath our conscious awareness, yet it powerfully shapes our behaviours and emotional responses. It stems from the layered architecture of the mind, first explored by Sigmund Freud and later expanded by Carl Jung, whose work laid the foundation for understanding the conscious, subconscious (pre-conscious), and unconscious aspects of human psychology. Their pioneering theories, now supported by modern psychology, reveal how unhealed trauma and early childhood conditioning can create internal patterns that continue to influence us long after the original experience has passed.

To heal stress at its roots, we must understand the **construct of the human mind**, the origin of our emotional responses, and how trauma disables our adult capacity to navigate life with clarity and presence.

By learning how the **Id, Ego, and Superego** function in conversations, and how they distort authentic expression, we begin the journey of integrating the parts of your mind.

When **neuroscience-based practices** are incorporated (activating the prefrontal cortex and calming the amygdala), we can rewire habitual stress responses or coping mechanisms developed in former years. But more on that in later chapters.

When the **Higher Self** is invited into dialogue, communication becomes a pathway for healing, not just survival.

THE THREE LAYERS OF THE MIND: FREUD'S CLASSIC MODEL

Freud described the human psyche as made up of three main components:

1. The Id (The Inner Child)

- Instinctive, emotional, impulsive
- Seeks pleasure and avoids pain
- Reacts to unmet needs or desires.

This part of the mind is present at birth and does not mature. It wants what it wants, NOW. The Id (Inner Child) is responsible for our raw emotional responses and is where trauma often roots itself. The Inner Child operates entirely from the subconscious and feels deeply, but cannot analyse or reason.

2. The Superego (The Internalised Inner Parent)

- Critical, moralising, rule-bound
- Voice of societal, familial, or cultural expectations
- Origin of guilt, shame, and perfectionism.

The Superego (Inner Parent) is formed during childhood, based on how we were raised, disciplined, and loved. It carries the inner critic and the emotional inheritance of our caregivers. When overactive, it is harsh, rigid, and self-punishing.

3. The Ego (The Rational Adult/Inner Adult/Adult Self)

- Mediates between the Id and Super ego (Inner Child and Inner Parent)
- Operates from reality, reason, and conscious decision-making
- Ideally grounded, discerning, and aligned with truth.

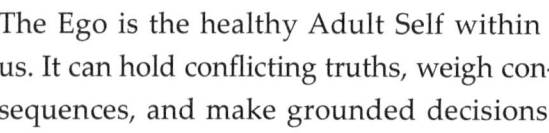

The Ego is the healthy Adult Self within us. It can hold conflicting truths, weigh consequences, and make grounded decisions. However, when trauma is present, especially in specific areas (like relationships, finances, or self-worth), the Adult Self voice becomes silenced. In these areas, the emotional reactions of the Inner Child and the judgment of the Inner Parent dominate.

THE ABSENCE OF THE ADULT SELF VOICE IN TRAUMATISED AREAS

If trauma occurred in a particular area of your life, for example, you were emotionally neglected as a child, then your Adult Self voice may be "offline" in that specific context. That means:

- In romantic relationships, you may react from your Inner Child (fear of abandonment, neediness, anxiety)
- In your career, you may respond from the Inner Parent (self-criticism, perfectionism, fear of failure).

Without the rational, emotionally balanced Adult Self to mediate, these areas of life are governed by emotional reactivity and limiting beliefs. This creates **stress**, not because the present situation is dangerous, but because the mind is referencing unresolved past pain as if it's happening now.

Example:

> You ask for help and receive a delayed response. Your Inner Child, who equates delayed responses with rejection, panics. The Inner Parent criticises: *"You're being needy."* The Adult Self, who would calmly assess the situation and maybe send a follow-up message, is absent.

This is how stress becomes internalised and magnified.

JUNG'S CONTRIBUTION: THE SHADOW AND THE COLLECTIVE UNCONSCIOUS

While Freud focused on individual parts of the mind, Carl Jung introduced the concept of **archetypes** and the **collective unconscious**, the inherited, universal blueprint for human behaviour.

Archetypes include:

- The Child
- The Parent
- The Hero
- The Shadow (repressed aspects of the self).

Jung emphasised that many of our emotional patterns are inherited and that the **Shadow**; parts of ourselves we deny or suppress, holds the very emotions we struggle to manage.

When the Adult Self voice is weak or absent, we often fall into **Shadow behaviour:** emotional outbursts, avoidance, people-pleasing, or control. These are distorted attempts to manage inner chaos when the conscious mind can no longer regulate the emotional tension.

INNER VOICES IN DIALOGUE: HOW STRESS MANIFESTS

We often only hear two voices speaking, when we actually have four voices within ourself. When your stress spikes, ask: Who is speaking right now? Which voice is missing?

Inner Voice	Triggered by...	Typical Dialogue	Emotional Outcome
Inner Child	Unmet needs, abandonment	"No one cares about me."	Anxiety, panic
Inner Parent	Failure, imperfection	"You should have done better."	Shame, guilt
Adult Self	Truth and clarity	"Let's assess what really happened."	Grounded calm
Higher Self (Soul)	Intuition, values	"You are safe. You are loved."	Peace, insight

HOW TRAUMA SILENCES THE ADULT SELF

If you've been hurt, humiliated, or neglected in a particular area, the Adult Self does not feel safe operating there. It defers to the protective strategies of the Inner Child and Inner Parent.

In trauma:

- The **Inner Child** seeks safety through avoidance, clinging, or regression
- The **Inner Parent** enforces control through criticism, pressure, or fear
- The **Adult Self** retreats, overwhelmed by the emotional storm.

The body experiences this as stress. The mind spins in rumination. Emotions flood the nervous system. There is no internal safety.

The irony is that the very part of us (the Adult Self) that can assess, calm, and heal the situation is missing.

When trauma or emotional overwhelm occurs at a young age, especially when no external adult is present to help us regulate or make sense of it, the Adult Self within us doesn't fully form in that area. As a result, the Inner Child's unmet needs, and the Inner Parent's internalised criticism, continue to dominate the scene. Until now, this may have been unconscious. But you're starting to see: your stress is not just about pressure from the outside world. It's about the disconnection *within you*.

REALIGNMENT: REBUILDING THE INTERNAL ADULT SELF

To address stress at its root, we must:

1. **Acknowledge Which Voice Is Active** – Name the voice that's reacting (e.g., *"My Inner Child is scared."*)
2. **Regulate the Nervous System** – Use breath, grounding, or movement to re-engage the body or other healing techniques and clearing
3. **Activate the Adult Self** – Ask: What would a wise, calm version of me do?
4. **Bring in the Higher Self** – Reconnect with values, intuition, and soul truth.

Over time, this process rebuilds the Adult Self voice in areas where it has been silenced. This is how healing becomes possible and stress no longer runs the show.

Understanding the architecture of your mind, the interplay between the Inner Child, Inner Parent, and Adult Self, gives you the foundational awareness to see how your stress responses are not random. They are structured. Predictable. Conditioned.

THE PSYCHIC APPARATUS (ID, EGO, SUPEREGO) IN COMMUNICATION

The Id (Inner Child), Ego (Adult Self), and Superego (Inner Parent) are not just static concepts to be studied. They are active energies that influence how we speak, listen, and react in every interaction.

They exist in a dynamic tension within the psyche, moving **between the conscious, preconscious, and unconscious realms.**

In conversation, these voices can either create trust and connection or trigger defensiveness, projection, and shutdown.

Your communication becomes soul-guided when you bring conscious awareness to **who is speaking;** the wounded Inner Child, the fearful manager (the Adult Self) or the inner critic (Inner Parent). Through consistent practice, you retrain your mind and body to express your true essence, rather than your old survival patterns.

HOW EACH LEVEL INFLUENCES THE WORDS YOU CHOOSE, YOUR TONE, YOUR BODY LANGUAGE

The Id (Inner Child) in Communication

Expanded Understanding:

- The Inner Child speaks from raw, unmet needs. It seeks instant gratification, safety, and relief from emotional discomfort
- In dialogue, the Inner Child often **blurts out, interrupts, or escalates** when it feels unseen or unheard
- It doesn't consider consequences or tone, it simply reacts
- If triggered, the Inner Child can hijack a conversation with reactivity or regress into avoidance.

Examples in Communication:

- *"Why don't you ever listen to me?!"*
- *"Fine! Whatever. You don't care."*
- *"You always do this to me!"*
- Silent treatment or emotional withdrawal
- Over-explaining or over-apologising to soothe fear of rejection.

How Soul Work Transforms This:

- By calming the nervous system (through polyvagal techniques and other healing modalities), giving the Inner Child a voice outside of the trigger moment, and inviting the Adult Self to hold space, the Inner Child's impulsivity is softened.

The Ego (Adult Self) in Communication

Expanded Understanding:

- The Adult Self tries to **keep us safe** and functional by managing image, controlling outcomes, and maintaining a sense of identity
- In conversation, the Adult Self often **tries to negotiate** between the demands of the Inner Child and the prohibitions of the Inner Parent
- The Adult Self can become hyper-rational, losing emotional authenticity in its attempt to "get it right" and it may lean into perfectionism, people-pleasing, conflict avoidance, or overthinking when under pressure.

Examples in Communication:

- *"I'm fine, don't worry about me."* (hiding real feelings)
- *"Let me explain exactly why I did that..."* (over-explaining)
- *"What's the safest thing to say here?"* (walking on eggshells)
- Obsessing about how one came across after the conversation.

How Soul Work Transforms This:

- The Adult Self learns to pause, breathe, access the prefrontal cortex, and choose from **authentic presence**, not reactive management.

The Superego (Inner Parent) in Communication

Expanded Understanding:

- The Inner Parent polices conversations with internalised "shoulds," **moral judgment, punishments and shame**
- It often shames you during or after interactions for being "too much," "not enough," "wrong," or "selfish"
- It can also project these judgments onto others, making conversations feel cold, superior, or guilt-ridden.

Examples in Communication:

- *"You shouldn't have said that. Now they think you're foolish."*
- *"You're too emotional. No one likes that."*
- *"Why can't they be more considerate? People should know better."*
- *"It's selfish to set that boundary."*

How Soul Work Transforms This:

- Through conscious awareness and compassion, the Inner Parent is softened
- The voice of the **Adult Self** becomes louder than the Inner Parent's internalised critic
- The nervous system is trained to **de-fuse** from shame triggers.

The Higher Self in Communication

At the heart of this journey back to your authentic voice lies the Higher

Self. Your soul's wisdom, untouched by trauma, conditioning, or egoic distortion. It is not another part of the personality like the Inner Child or the Inner Parent; it is your truest, most expansive self, beyond wounding, beyond fear. It is the voice of your wholeness.

Unlike the impulsive demands of the Inner Child, the managing strategies of the Adult Self, or the critical commands of the Inner Parent, the Higher Self speaks quietly and steadily from a place of compassion, clarity, and knowing.

When you speak from your Higher Self, you speak from a place of presence. You communicate from love, not from fear.

How the Higher Self Speaks to Your Adult Self:

- The Higher Self does not rush. Its guidance comes through stillness, intuition, and a deep inner knowing
- It does not demand, criticise, or defend
- It honours truth, yet delivers it with kindness
- It is never laced with guilt or shame
- It sees the sacredness in both self and others, even in moments of conflict.

How to Recognise When the Higher Self is Speaking:

- Your body is calm. Breath is steady
- There is no internal urgency or "push" to speak
- There is no attachment to outcome, only the desire for authentic expression
- The words feel spacious, generous, and respectful.

How to Recognise When It Is NOT the Higher Self:

- The voice feels harsh, tight, demanding, superior, or shaming (Inner Parent)
- The voice feels impulsive, needy, blaming, defensive, or dra-

- matic (Inner Child)
- The voice feels confused, indecisive or directionless (Adult Self)
- The body is tense, the voice is strained, and the breath is shallow
- The nervous system is dysregulated. Fight, flight, freeze, or fawn is activated.

What The Higher Self Sounds Like in Communication to the Adult Self:

- "I hear how this feels for you. Here's what is true for me."
- "This matters to me. And I respect that it may land differently for you."
- "I choose to honour my boundary with love and clarity."
- "There is no right or wrong here. This is my experience."
- "Even though this is hard, I can stay open."
- "Right now, I need some space to return to calm, and then I'd like to continue this conversation."
- "I can hear how important this is to you. I'm listening, and I also want to be honest about how this feels for me."
- "I intend to stay connected, even if we see this differently."
- "I can honour your perspective, and I also need to honour my truth."
- "It's okay that we're both feeling tender here. I can hold that with compassion."
- "I am allowed to speak my needs, even if it disappoints someone else."
- "I trust that expressing my truth with kindness serves both of us. Even if it's uncomfortable."

How to Strengthen the Adult Self's Voice in Dialogue:

- **Pause before responding**: invite the Higher Self forward, *"What would love say here?"*
- **Notice the body:** Are you in calm presence, or in survival response?
- **Practice conscious breathing:** Regulating the nervous system so the Higher Self can be heard over the noise of fear
- **Reflect on conversations after the fact:** Where did you speak from love or from wounded parts? This builds awareness
- **Engage in daily practices** (meditation, soul dialogue, grounding) to strengthen your Higher Self's presence in your life. Then it will show up more often in your voice.

THE GIFT OF THE HIGHER SELF IN COMMUNICATION

When you speak from the Adult Self with the guidance of the Higher Self, you create a field of resonance. The conversation itself becomes a space of healing, both for you and for those with whom you engage. You stop reinforcing old patterns of shame, blame, and fear. You begin transmitting love, clarity, and truth. Dialogue becomes a sacred act.

And most importantly, you begin to **reprogram the subconscious mind** through repeated, soul-aligned expression. Each time you choose this voice over the reactive voices, you **rewire your inner architecture** toward presence, peace, and authenticity.

Remember, though, you are not trying to "be the Higher Self" perfectly. You are remembering who you already are. The goal is not to banish the Inner Child or Inner

Parent, but to lead with the Higher Self, with compassion for the parts still healing. Every time you *catch a moment of reaction and choose the Higher Self instead*, you are rewiring your nervous system and subconscious. However, more details will be provided in subsequent chapters on how to identify and follow the guidance of your Higher Self.

How the Higher Self Corresponds to the Brain

When you are in **fight-flight-freeze (sympathetic nervous system)**, the amygdala is activated, it floods the body with stress hormones, this is when the Inner Child and Inner Parent hijack communication.

When you access the **Higher Self** via the **Adult Self**, you are helping shift brain activity into the **prefrontal cortex**, the part of your brain responsible for conscious choice, empathy, compassion, and long-term thinking.

Practices that support this shift include:

- Slow, diaphragmatic breathing
- Grounding techniques (feet on floor, hand on heart)
- Mindful pauses before responding
- Reflective inquiry (*"Who is speaking right now?"*)
- Visualisation of the Higher Self as an inner guide.

Over time, the more you **choose Higher Self** responses, the more you rewire your neural pathways, increasing **vagal tone** and your capacity for **soul-aligned communication even under stress**. However, neuroscience-based rewiring can significantly accelerate this process, creating the conscious pathways sought to stabilise your system, but more on this later.

INNER VOICE MAP FOR CONSCIOUS

THE ARCHITECTURE OF STRESS

CONVERSATIONS - SPOTTING THE VOICE IN CONVERSATIONS

One of the most potent ways to begin shifting the architecture of stress within us is by becoming aware of which parts of ourselves are speaking, both in conversations with others and in the silent dialogue we carry within.

Too often, it is the Inner Child, the Inner Parent, or the protective Inner Parent managing our words and tone, without us even realising it. But the more often we pause to reflect on which voice was leading, and gently invite the Higher Self to speak instead, the more we rewire these old patterns and bring our communication into proper alignment.

Use the following Voice Awareness Journal Page after conversations or emotionally charged moments. You are not seeking perfection, only greater awareness, so that more and more of your voice may come from your wholeness.

HIGHER SELF

ADULT SELF

INNER PARENT

INNER CHILD

INVITING THE HIGHER SELF TO LEAD YOUR VOICE

Before stepping into any conversation that holds emotional charge, whether it's a boundary to set, a truth to express, or a misunderstanding to mend, it can be deeply supportive to pause and reconnect with your Higher Self.

The following reflection will help you settle your body, soften reactive voices, and invite your soul's wisdom to guide your words. You can practice this quietly before a conversation or take a few breaths to anchor these intentions throughout your day.

Try the four D's before responding:

- **Delay** so you can bring awareness into your Adult Self
- **Decode** what your Inner Child and Inner Parent is asking for
- **Decide** on the best path forward with advice from your Higher Self
- **Deliver** the new direction forward including setting boundaries where needed.

Keep on reading to learn how hear the Adult and Higher Self.

Before / During / After a Conversation:

Here's a sample Completed Voice Awareness Journal Page:

Conversation Moment	Who Was Speaking?	What Was I Feeling?	Was I Reacting or Choosing?	What Would Higher Self Say Here?
Discussing unmet needs with my partner	Inner Child	Hurt, abandoned, defensive	Reacting	"I can express my needs calmly without blame."
Responding to feedback from my colleague	Inner Parent	Shame, self-criticism	Reacting	"Their feedback does not define my worth."
Setting a boundary with a family member	Adult Self	Calm, clear, compassionate	Choosing	"I honour this boundary with love and respect."

~

You've now seen the inner architecture, the voices, patterns, and layers that shape how you think, feel, and communicate. And while understanding this inner framework is a crucial starting point, insight alone is not enough. Awareness must become embodied. And old patterns must be brought to light, not through force, but through loving, conscious practice.

Neuroscience-based tools can help accelerate this process; we will explore them soon. But before we move into techniques, we need to go deeper. Because beneath every old belief, every reactive pattern, every place where your voice has been hijacked... lives a message, one your system is trying to send you.

Stress, as you will soon see, is not your enemy. It is your body's messenger. And when we learn how to hear it rather than fear it, stress becomes one of our greatest teachers on the road back to Self.

Let's step into that wisdom, together, in the next chapter.

REFLECTION & INTEGRATION

Reflection Prompt - "Who's Speaking for Me?"

As you move through daily conversations, begin asking:

"Who is speaking for me right now?"

- Is it the wounded Inner Child seeking safety or validation?
- Is it the critical Inner Parent enforcing shame or control?
- Is it the Adult Self trying to manage the moment, keep peace, or fix?
- Or is it the Higher Self; clear, calm, grounded in truth?

Journal Prompt - Mapping My Voices

Choose a recent emotionally charged moment or conversation.

Now reflect and write:

- What happened?
- What did I feel in my body?
- What thoughts or inner dialogue came up?
- Which voice do I believe was most active?
- Which voice was missing?
- What might my Higher Self have said or done differently?

Realignment Practice - Rewriting the Inner Dialogue

Take a moment to write compassionate replies from your Adult Self and Higher Self to any dominant Inner Child or Inner Parent beliefs you noticed.

Example:

- Inner Child: *"I'm not safe to speak up."*
- Adult Self: *"That fear makes sense, but we're safe now."*
- Higher Self: *"Your voice matters. You're safe to speak truth with love."*

Awareness Integration - End-of-Day Voice Check-In

Each evening, ask yourself:

- Who led my conversations today? Fear, control, or compassion?
- How did I feel before, during, and after key interactions?
- What intention can I carry forward tomorrow to invite my Higher Self to guide my voice more often?

Inviting the Higher Self to Lead My Voice (Daily Reflection)

Find a quiet space. Sit comfortably. Allow your hands to rest softly. Close your eyes if you wish. Begin to breathe gently, slowly, and entirely, in through the nose, out through the mouth.

With each breath, allow your body to settle…
… softening the shoulders…
… releasing the jaw…
… grounding your feet.

Now bring to mind the conversation you are preparing for. See the person (or people) you will be speaking with. Feel the energy of this interaction in your body, without judgment, just noticing.

Now, gently ask yourself:

1. **Pause. Breathe** deeply.
2. **Ask:** "Who do I want to speak for me in this moment? My fear, my wounded Inner Child, my inner critic…or the wise, compassionate voice of my Higher Self?"
3. **Hand on heart. Breathe again. Say:** "I call on the deepest truth within me, the part of me that sees with love, speaks with clarity, and honours both self and other."
4. **Intention:** "Let my words today be shaped not by fear, but by compassion. Let me listen with curiosity. Let me speak with kindness. Let me remember that we are both whole beings, doing our best."
5. **Pause. Breathe.** Feel this alignment settling in your body.
6. **Breathe.** Begin your conversation with presence.
7. When you are ready, open your eyes, carrying this awareness into your conversation.

5

STRESS ISN'T THE PROBLEM – IT'S THE MESSAGE

You don't heal by becoming someone new. You heal by remembering who you were before the world taught you to be someone else.

Stress isn't the problem. It's the messenger. Beneath every anxious thought, every tightening in the chest, every wave of overwhelm, there is a more profound message waiting to be heard.

You now understand the inner architecture of your mind; its voices, its layers, and how each part colours your communication. But knowing the structure is only the beginning. The fundamental transformation begins when you learn to listen to what your inner world is trying to tell you, not just in words, but in sensations, emotions, and patterns as well. Because stress, at its core, is not your enemy. It is a message. A signal from your system that something is misaligned.

In this chapter, we will move from understanding structure into the heart of experience. We will explore how stress itself can become a powerful teacher, one that reveals exactly what within you is ready to be healed and reclaimed.

Stress is born not from the world outside, but from the dissonance within: when the wounded Inner Child, the rigid Inner Parent, and the silenced Adult Self battle for control. Now, we delve deeper into this emotional terrain. This is where theory becomes lived experience, where structure becomes sensation.

Stress, as we've come to understand, is not the enemy. It is a signal. A message. A call from within that something is misaligned.

> *Stress is never just about what's happening.*
> *It's about what's unhealed, unspoken,*
> *and unmet within you.*

THE EMOTIONAL BATTLE BENEATH THE SURFACE

Stress, for most people, feels like a symptom of too much, too many responsibilities, too much chaos, too much noise, too many demands, expectations or pressure. But stress is not simply the result of the world around you. More often, it's the manifestation of a deeper battle happening *within you*.

But if we peel back the layers, we often discover that stress is the manifestation of unresolved emotional conflict, not between you and the world, but between the parts of you that want different things.

This battle, this inner conflict, is the collision of opposing internal voices. Your conditioned fears wrestle with your emerging desires. Your Inner Child's fear of abandonment crashes into your Adult Self's logic and intentions. And your Inner Parent, trying to maintain control, employs outdated survival strategies or punishing methods, such as guilt, perfectionism, and criticism.

This collision is not just exhausting. It's destabilising. It creates the psychic friction that feels like anxiety, tension, emotional flooding, or numbness.

In this chapter, we go deeper into the emotional misalignments that create the psychic tension you feel as stress. We'll explore the difference between natural and distorted emotions, how your nervous system reacts to perceived threats from old conditioning, and how your belief systems, formed during moments of early trauma, become the silent architects of your reactivity.

We're no longer looking at the blueprint. We're entering the lived experience of it.

TWO EMOTIONAL LANGUAGES: NATURAL AND DISTORTED

We each hold within us two distinct emotional languages:

- **Natural emotions**, which arise from present-moment awareness, aligned values, and authentic self-expression
- **Distorted emotions**, which are reactions rooted in fear, past conditioning, unresolved trauma, and fear-based beliefs.

These distorted emotions are the mind's survival responses, automatic reactions designed to keep us safe. But they often hijack our capacity to choose consciously. They make us believe we are still living in the past, still under threat, and must act accordingly.

For example:

- Natural fear helps protect us. Distorted fear becomes anxiety, paranoia, or panic
- Natural love is nurturing and open. Distorted love becomes controlling, needy, or fearful of abandonment

- Natural anger sets healthy boundaries. Distorted anger can explode in rage or collapse into powerlessness.

These reactions are the Inner Child's cries for safety: and the Inner Parent's need for protection. And when there's no grounded Adult Self voice to mediate, the distorted emotions take over. Especially when unresolved stress prevails, you'll find yourself responding in distorted emotions side of the table below.

THE NATURAL EMOTIONS VS DISTORTED EMOTIONS TABLE:

	NATURAL EMOTIONS	DISTORTED EMOTIONS
FEAR	Fight/Flight/Freeze impulse, cautious, startled	Greed, obstinate, suspicious, overcautious, frightened, worry, anxious, petrified, panicked and phobias
LOVE	Blissful, self-confident, giving and receiving, kindness, nurturing, emotional support and self-love	Controlling, demanding, possessive, abandoned, and dominating, inadequate, insecure, instability of love.
ANGER	Used to bring about change, self protects, assertive and firm with self and others	Rage, hatred, frustrated, bitterness, self-hate, resentment, aggressive, hurt, powerless, no inner authority, defeated, cheated and intimidated.
JEALOUS	Impels and motivates us to grow, improve our self worth, model from another person's behaviour	Envious, deceitful, criticism of self and others, competitive and comparative
GRIEF	Sharing of feelings, loss and tears	Depression, blame, regret, remorse, guilty, self-pity, martyrdom or suicidal

STRESS AS A SYMPTOM OF EMOTIONAL MISALIGNMENT

Stress doesn't just come from long to-do lists or pressure at work or home. At its core, **stress is a form of emotional misalignment.**

It is the result of living in contradiction to your inner truth. It's the friction that arises when:

- You say *"Yes"* when you want to say *"No"*
- You silence your needs to avoid confrontation
- You perform a version of yourself to gain love or approval.

And when your **subconscious programming**, the beliefs you adopted early in life, clashes with your current awareness, **inner conflict erupts.** Your body tenses. Your mind races. Emotions rise and twist into distortion. That's when you begin to feel emotionally flooded, confused, or numb. You may even hear conflicting thoughts in your mind, like two opposing forces fighting for control.

This is precisely what the old "angel and devil on your shoulders" metaphor describes, an internal battle between the part of you that is trying to keep you safe and the part that is trying to help you grow.

This dissonance causes stress not because of what is happening externally, but because of the internal contradiction. You are betraying your truth to maintain an identity that was formed for survival, not wholeness.

THE VULNERABILITY OF CHILDHOOD PROGRAMMING

Before the age of seven, a child's rational brain, the prefrontal cortex, is not fully developed. This means that during those formative years, everything you experience is taken as fact. Every comment, every look, every emotional withdrawal, every explosion of rage, all of it gets stored as absolute truth.

If someone tells you *"You're too much"* or withdraws love when you cry, your young mind doesn't analyse the situation. It doesn't say, *"Mum must be having a bad day"* or *"Dad never learned emotional regulation."* It says: *"There's something wrong with me."*

These become emotional truths, and they form the software your subconscious uses to navigate the world. Until those beliefs are challenged, healed, or reframed, they continue to run silently beneath the surface, dictating how you feel, think, and behave.

And where trauma has occurred in a specific area of life, such as relationships, identity, or self-worth, the Adult Self voice often fails to form fully in that realm. Instead of stepping in to soothe or guide, the Adult Self becomes silent. The Inner Child, overwhelmed and unsupported, reacts with fear, shame, or a sense of neediness. Meanwhile, the Inner Parent may step in, but only with criticism, judgment, or pressure to conform. This creates a vacuum of leadership in the mind. And **without** a mature, calm, grounded Adult Self voice to mediate the emotional storm, stress escalates.

THE SUBCONSCIOUS SCRIPTS YOU INHERITED

Now think about it: How many times in your life have you been shown how to live in natural emotions? How many people, especially in childhood, modelled emotional health, regulation, or self-awareness?

Probably very few.

Instead, we are often exposed to distorted emotions from a young age, as very few of us were shown how to express natural emotions as children. Family conflict, suppressed anger, parental stress, jealousy between siblings, controlling behaviours, co-dependency, volatility, avoidance or emotional shutdowns, these become the emotional language we absorb and become our emotional scripts. These patterns are normalised in our world, so we adopt them, learning to react from fear, insecurity, and protection instead of presence and clarity.

In a world where love is conditional, emotions are unstable, and safety feels uncertain, we learn to survive rather than thrive.

And even though you were born whole, emotionally attuned, and deeply connected to your natural self, that connection was conditioned out of you. You were taught, often unintentionally, that distorted emotions are reality, and from there, the internal chaos begins.

And because the rational brain (the Adult Self) isn't entirely online in early childhood, everything we observed was absorbed as truth. If a parent withdrew love when we cried, we learned that vulnerability is unsafe. If we were criticised for failure, we equated mistakes with shame.

These subconscious scripts are still running. And in areas where trauma occurred, the Adult Self doesn't show up. Instead, the Inner Child reacts. The Inner Parent criticises. The Adult Self retreats. And stress ensues.

When the emotional storm hits, the body enters survival mode. The amygdala takes over, bypassing reason and rushing to safety. In this mode:

- Logic disappears
- Distorted beliefs resurface
- Emotional reactivity spikes.

You're not thinking, you're defending. And often, you're protecting against a ghost from the past. A memory. A belief. A pain that still lives in your nervous system.

STRESS AND THE SURVIVAL BRAIN

When stress hits, your body defaults to what it knows: survival mode. And in survival mode, the amygdala, your emotional brain, takes over. It doesn't ask, *"Is this logical?"* or *"Is this aligned with my values?"* It says:

"Get safe. Now."

Suppose your subconscious has linked conflict, rejection, or emotional exposure to past pain. In that case, your mind will do everything it can to avoid it, including hijacking your present-moment awareness with distorted emotions.

The internal message becomes: *I'm not safe. I'm powerless. I must protect myself at all costs.*

The more you let distorted emotions drive your decisions, the more stuck you feel, caught in loops of self-sabotage, avoidance, overreaction, or emotional shutdown. And this is the opposite of growth. It is stagnation masked as self-protection.

AUTHENTICITY IS THE ANTIDOTE

The way out isn't suppression or avoidance. It's **authenticity**. Your soul is always guiding you back to presence. It's always nudging you toward truth, wholeness, and authenticity. But authenticity isn't always easy.

To live authentically is to stop performing and start being. It's not perfection. It's **congruence**. Aligning your actions, words, and choices with your true self. It requires that you **stand alone** at times, that you release the masks, and that you accept your own complexity, even when others don't. To live authentically is to speak truthfully, feel honestly, and act congruently, even when it's hard. It's about releasing the performance and returning to presence. This often requires letting go of the roles you were taught to play: the peacemaker, the achiever, the rescuer, the obedient child.

But in doing so, you reclaim yourself.

And yes, this can feel lonely at first. But on the path of truth, you begin to find others walking beside you. People who are also unlearning, healing, and becoming real.

REWIRING THE SUBCONSCIOUS

The subconscious doesn't care about truth. It cares about safety. That's why your responses are often outdated. But by naming your beliefs, meeting your emotions with compassion, and reintroducing the Adult Self voice, you begin to rewire the system.

This isn't about forcing positivity. It's about witnessing your truth without judgment.

When you've stored negative experiences, limiting beliefs, and unresolved emotions in the subconscious, living daily with natural emotions can feel almost impossible. Your inner world becomes automated. The subconscious takes over like a well-trained driver. And unless you consciously interrupt it, it will continue to steer your life based on outdated maps.

Ironically, the subconscious believes it's keeping you safe. If experience has taught you that vulnerability leads to pain, you will work hard to avoid any situation that even remotely resembles that. But this also prevents you from growing, connecting, and fully living.

Learning how the mind works, how it stores emotion, how it creates beliefs, how its voices and agendas play out, gives you the power to change.

This isn't about "fixing" yourself. It's about **understanding yourself**.

When you begin to see the origin of your emotional reactions, you gain the ability to respond differently. And that's where freedom begins.

WHEN JUSTIFIED EMOTIONS ARE STILL MISALIGNED

When past references and beliefs trigger our emotions, it's easy to feel *justified* in those emotions, even if they're distorted. Depending on your unique conditioning, you'll respond with either natural or distorted emotions based on how your subconscious has stored previous experiences.

This is where inner conflict deepens: your current environment may not be unsafe, but your mind is still referencing a past where it was.

I often use this metaphor with clients: *"If someone gives you a bunch of flowers, how do you feel?"* Most will say loved, special, grateful. But the truth is, the act itself is neutral. Someone handed over a bunch of flowers. What causes the emotional reaction isn't the act itself, but the reference it triggers in your mind.

If you've received flowers in the past as an apology after being hurt, you might feel sceptical. If they remind you of a parent's love, you may feel a warm sense of affection. If they triggered a memory of loss, you might even feel grief. The meaning you give the act **comes from your conditioning**, not from the act itself.

In truth, no one gives you love, pain, or validation. They perform actions, and those actions trigger emotions *within you*. These are your internal responses, shaped by your personal history, your beliefs, and your emotional wiring. Different people will respond to the same situation in very different ways because they are referencing different inner stories.

So, when someone triggers a deep emotional response in you, whether it's anger, rejection, or sadness, it's often not about the current moment at all. It's about **the stored belief** system that's been poked. This is what we refer to as "someone poking the bear." That bear is the unhealed wound. And once triggered, we often justify our emotions without questioning whether they're actually in alignment with our true selves.

LAYERING EMOTION TO STAY SAFE

Because unresolved beliefs and old emotions live in the subconscious, your mind searches for past references in milliseconds. As soon as a situation resembles a prior threat, it pulls up a stored reaction and **fires it off automatically.** Your nervous system is not assessing truth. It's assessing risk.

And this is how we begin layering distorted emotions. We feel misaligned, but instead of recognising the wound beneath, we try to control the situation:

- We demand love to soothe abandonment
- We lash out to avoid feeling powerless
- We withdraw to escape potential rejection.

What we're doing is trying to stay safe, to **control the outer environment** so we don't have to feel our inner discomfort. And when we can't control what's around us, we begin controlling ourselves the way others once did, through criticism, shame, and suppression. This is how the **internalised critical Inner Parent** is formed. Not nurturing, not supportive, but judgmental and punishing.

Over time, this self-abandonment leads to psychic tension. A kind of emotional knot between who you are and who you think you must be to survive.

WHEN COPING BECOMES NUMBING

When you don't know how to soothe yourself in alignment with your true self, the internal conflict doesn't go away, it gets buried. And so, we turn to numbing:

- **Workaholism** to avoid sitting still
- **Alcohol, drugs, or prescription medication** to dull emotional overwhelm
- **Addictive behaviours** like gambling, compulsive sex, or bingeing. Each one offering temporary relief from the voice of inner

disconnection.

These coping strategies are often judged harshly by society. But they are not moral failings, they are attempts to manage unbearable internal conflict. They are signs of someone trying to soothe what they were never taught to face.

And if not through numbing, we try distraction. We keep busy. We scroll, we hustle, we stay one step ahead of the emotion we fear will catch us. But distraction is not healing. It is simply a delay.

WHY THINKING ALONE CAN'T HEAL YOU

Talk therapy, psychology, and counselling can be incredibly helpful in understanding what happened to you. They offer structure, insight, and language to your story. But they also have limitations.

Many talk-based modalities engage the **thinking mind**, helping clients analyse, rationalise, and reflect. But healing doesn't happen in the mind alone. If you're only thinking *about* your pain, you're staying in your head, and avoiding the very emotions that need to be felt and released.

This is the trap of intellectualising trauma. You understand *why* something happened, but you still feel stuck. That's because the healing work hasn't yet reached the **emotional root** where the belief was formed.

To truly reprogram the mind, you must allow the **emotional body** to speak. You must trace your reaction to the feeling, then to the belief beneath it, and then to the moment it began. And only from there can you release and replace it.

THE REAL WORK OF EMOTIONAL HEALING

Most people move through life toggling between natural and distorted emotions, unaware they're slipping in and out of their power. This is entirely normal.

The key to transformation is becoming **conscious of when it happens**.

Pay attention to the moments where you feel disconnected, reactive, or "not yourself." Those are the places where you've handed your power to a past belief.

Start asking:

- *Where am I slipping into distortion?*
- *What old belief is driving this reaction?*
- *What do I need to feel safe enough to respond differently?*

Living in your **natural emotional state**, even amid pain, restores your sense of self. Because natural emotions are congruent with your essence, they move through you, rather than bind you.

Distorted emotions, on the other hand, are like static. They interfere with clarity, communication, and inner peace. And yet, they can be the very guideposts that point you back to what needs to be healed.

WHEN THE MIND CAN NO LONGER HOLD THE PAIN

There are times when the internal conflict between who we are and who we've been conditioned to be becomes so intense, so unrelenting, that the human mind can no longer maintain balance. This prolonged psychic tension, where distorted beliefs, unresolved trauma, emotional suppression, and chronic disconnection collide, can cause the mind to fracture under the weight. In some individuals, this leads to psychosis, a break from reality where thoughts become disorganised, perception distorts, and the inner and outer worlds blur. For others, the pain of feeling chronically unseen, unloved, or unsafe can create a sense of emotional implosion, where the only perceived escape is to end the suffering entirely.

Suicidal thoughts are not weakness.[1] They are a symptom of a mind that has been fighting too long without relief, a soul overwhelmed by its internal emotional storm. The tragedy is that those who reach this point often don't want to die; they don't know how to keep living with the pain they're carrying. This is why awareness, compassion, and emotional healing are not luxuries, they are lifelines. Reaching out for help, speaking the unspoken, and gently unpacking those layers of suffering is a courageous act of survival and rebirth. No matter how dark the path has been, healing is always possible when we bring truth, presence, and support to the parts of ourselves that feel lost.

HEALING COMES THROUGH RECOGNITION

What I find in nearly every client I work with is this: beneath the surface, the root belief is almost always one of three things:

- *I am not good enough*
- *I am not lovable*
- *I am not worthy.*

These core wounds often stem from simple moments in childhood. Being left alone, being overlooked, facing something frightening, or feeling unwanted. And while the situation might seem minor to an adult mind, to a young child with no rational filter, **it becomes law**.

The key to healing is recognising that **you created these beliefs**. Someone else's behaviour may have prompted them, but the belief itself was formed in your mind.

That means you have the power to change it.

You can only remove what you are willing to see. When you observe yourself reacting in distorted ways; demanding love, overcompensating, shrinking in fear, you're being given an invitation to heal. You're seeing the exact pattern that has kept you stuck.

And in seeing it clearly, you begin to dissolve its power.

Remember, most people don't live entirely in distorted or natural emotions. They oscillate. The goal is not perfection. It's awareness.

Start noticing:

- *When am I triggered?*
- *Which part of me is reacting?*
- *What belief is driving this?*

Then respond from the Adult Self. Offer the Inner Child compassion. Reassure the Inner Parent. Invite the Higher Self in.

This is integration. This is alignment. This is healing.

~

Now that you can recognise stress not as a threat, but as a message from within, you have a powerful opening to meet yourself differently. This is the beginning of emotional fluency. Learning to listen beneath the noise to the truth of what your system is really asking for.

REFLECTION & INTEGRATION

Self-Reconnection Practice:

> *Healing doesn't come from erasing who you've been. It comes from embracing who you are becoming.*

Take a moment to check in with yourself. Inner conflict often whispers in your reactions, your stress, and your sense of disconnection. But it can also become the gateway to your most significant transformation.

Reflect on the following questions in your journal or quiet time:

- Which of my emotional reactions feel "justified" but still leave me disempowered? What belief might be driving those reactions?

- Where in my life am I currently experiencing the most inner conflict?
- Are the emotions I feel in these situations natural (present, grounded) or distorted (fear-based, reactive)?
- Can I trace these reactions back to earlier beliefs or childhood conditioning?
- What version of me do I become when I'm trying to stay safe or earn love?
- What would my life look like if I trusted natural emotions as my compass instead of letting distorted emotions steer?

Realignment Practice:

The next time you're emotionally triggered, pause. Ask: *"Is this a natural emotion responding to the present, or a distorted emotion reacting to the past?"* Journal your answer. Observe without judgment.

This week, choose one recurring emotional reaction, something that regularly makes you feel powerless, angry, anxious, or unseen. Each time it surfaces, pause and ask:

"Is this emotion a reflection of my present truth? Or a memory from my past?"

Breathe. Give the emotion space to exist without judgment. Then gently invite a more natural emotion into the space. This is not about forcing joy. It's about choosing alignment, one honest shift at a time.

[1] *If You Are in Crisis or Feeling Overwhelmed*

If you or someone you know is struggling with suicidal thoughts or emotional distress, please know that you are not alone, and support is available:

- *Australia – Lifeline: 13 11 14 (lifeline.org.au)*
- *New Zealand – Lifeline: 0508 828 865 (lifeline.org.nz)*
- *United Kingdom – Samaritans: 116 123 (samaritans.org)*
- *United States – National Suicide & Crisis Lifeline: 988 (988lifeline.org)*
- *Canada – National Suicide & Crisis Lifeline: 988 (988.ca)*

If you're outside these countries, seek help from your local mental health services, hospital, or emergency line. There are people who care and want to walk alongside you. You do not have to face this alone.

Part II

When the Body Speaks Louder than Words

How your nervous system shapes your voice, reactions, and relationships.

This part is where science meets self-awareness. Your nervous system is not just a background process. It's the gatekeeper of your inner voices. Here, you'll learn how your breath, tone, and pace reveal exactly what state you're in, and how distorted emotions and reactive patterns override the true you. This is where you stop reacting… and start listening to your body, your breath, and your authentic voice beneath it all.

6

HOW YOUR NERVOUS SYSTEM SHAPES YOUR INNER DIALOGUE

The words that come out of your mouth are shaped first by the state of your nervous system, not by logic, not by intention, but by whether you feel safe enough to speak from your truth.

As we transition from the emotional foundations of childhood and trauma to the present-day experience of inner voice and nervous system response, this chapter marks the beginning of a practical inward journey. Here, you'll discover how your body speaks first, often before you even realise, and how that physical response shapes your inner world and the voices you hear. This is where awareness turns into transformation.

In the previous chapter, we began to see that stress is not the enemy. It is the messenger. And beneath every wave of stress lies an internal story: old beliefs, unhealed wounds, and emotional patterns shaped long before our conscious mind could understand them. But knowing these stories isn't enough. If we are to shift them truly, we must understand where they reside, not just in the mind, but in the body. Because long before a thought forms or a word is spoken, the body speaks first. It is your nervous system that decides whether you feel safe enough to access compassion... or if you will fall into the old reflexes of fear, defence, or withdrawal. If we are to change how we think, feel, and communicate, we must learn to work with the body's intelligence, not against it. That is the work ahead of us in this chapter.

YOUR BODY IS THE FIRST TO SPEAK

Your body is reacting to the past, even when your mind believes it is in the present.

One of the most essential truths in healing is this: your body speaks first. Long before the mind constructs a thought, your body is already responding. This is because your nervous system, which is fully integrated with your mind, is constantly wired to scan the environment for signs of safety or danger.

It does not operate on logic. It operates on survival. Based on your past experiences, and the emotions, beliefs, and meanings you attached to those experiences, your nervous system develops a "memory." It reacts first to what is happening around you, often before your conscious mind even recognises it. And in doing so, it dictates which voice becomes dominant inside you.

When your body perceives a threat, whether it is real or only perceived, it activates the fight, flight, or freeze response. If you carry unresolved emotional wounds or stored trauma, these old imprints will often cause the nervous system to react disproportionately to present situations. In these moments, your survival wiring takes over. Your Inner Child's voice may hijack your words. Your Inner Parent may start to criticise.

Your Adult Self may scramble to manage the threat. And your Higher Self, the calm, wise voice of truth, may not be heard at all.

In fight/flight, you perceive a threat, so you *hear* others as being more critical than they are. You interpret neutral tones as attacks. You interrupt or "over-explain" to protect yourself.

In **freeze**, you perceive helplessness, so you minimise *your voice*. You nod, agree, or say nothing to avoid conflict, even when you want to speak.

Why? Because when your nervous system is in survival mode, it is not interested in wisdom. It is interested in protection. Your body is reacting to the past, not the present. And until the system feels safe, your conscious Adult Self cannot lead, and your Higher Self's guidance remains muted beneath the noise of automatic reactions.

This is why **awareness of your nervous system state** is absolutely key. Without this awareness, you may spend most of your time speaking from a place of fight, flight, or freeze, defending against old wounds, rather than responding to what is actually here and now. The more you learn to **"gate-keep"** your state. To notice when your system is activated, the more you can choose to pause, regulate, and reconnect to the part of you that speaks from your soul.

THE MIND-BODY CONNECTION: ONE INTEGRATED SYSTEM

> *You cannot think your way into an authentic voice, you must feel safe enough to speak it.*

One of the most common misunderstandings in personal growth is the notion that the mind and body are separate systems, as though thoughts reside in one space and feelings in another. In truth, there is no such division. Your body and mind form **one integrated system**. They are in constant communication through your nervous system, vagus nerve, hormones, and electrical signals. What happens in your body is instantly mirrored in your mind, and what happens in your mind is felt through your body.

For some people, stress shows up first in the body: a tight chest, clenched jaw, racing heart, a rush of tension, often long before a conscious thought appears. For others, stress begins in the mind, characterised by racing thoughts, worry loops, and catastrophizing, which then trigger body sensations. Both pathways are equally valid. Either way, the experience always becomes a whole mind-body event.

This is why true healing and authentic communication, cannot happen in the mind alone. You cannot simply think your way into a calm, soul-aligned voice. You must also include the body. Until your nervous system feels safe, the higher centres of your mind, your conscious Adult Self and your Higher Self, cannot lead your communication.

When you honour this truth, that your body is not separate from your healing, but essential to it, you reclaim your power to change not only how you feel, but how you speak, connect, and live.

So if your nervous system is the first to speak, defaulting to reactive survival voices, the gateway through which all your inner voices and communication flow, how can you begin to work with it, rather than be ruled by it? The first step is understanding its map: how your system responds to a threat, how it signals safety, and how these states influence which parts of you are able to express. This is where the polyvagal map proves to be an invaluable guide.

HOW TO KNOW WHAT STATE YOU'RE IN (POLYVAGAL CUES LIST)

When you know your state, you regain choice.

Once you begin to understand how your nervous system shapes your voice and communication, the next step is learning to recognise, in the moment, what state you are actually in. The more you can feel these shifts in your body, the more choice you will have in how you speak and respond. Below is a simple guide to help you begin noticing your nervous system cues. Awareness is always the first doorway to change.

Ventral Vagal (Safe / Connected State):

- Breath is steady and full
- Shoulders are relaxed
- Jaw is soft
- Heart feels open, grounded
- Speech is calm, clear, and connected
- Able to listen with curiosity
- Words come with ease
- The Higher Self is accessible.

Sympathetic (Fight / Flight State):

- Breath is shallow or fast
- Heart racing or pounding
- Shoulders tight, jaw clenched
- Speech speeds up or becomes sharp
- Urge to control, defend, prove
- Difficult to listen fully
- Words feel urgent or forced
- Inner Child or Inner Parent dominate.

Dorsal Vagal (Freeze / Collapse State):

- Breath is flat, faint, or held

- Body feels heavy, slumped, disconnected
- Voice is soft, monotone, hesitant, or disappears
- Mind feels foggy or blank
- Difficult to access thoughts or words
- Desire to withdraw, hide, disappear
- Feelings of helplessness or numbness
- The Higher Self feels far away.

INNER DIALOGUE - HOW THE BODY SHAPES WHAT YOU TELL YOURSELF

Your inner voice is shaped by your body's state, not by who you truly are.

It is not only your words and tone that change with your nervous system state, **your inner dialogue shifts as well**. The body does not simply react outwardly; it also shapes what you say *to yourself* in those moments.

When your nervous system is calm and regulated, your inner voice tends to sound compassionate, spacious, and open to possibility. You are more likely to think: *"I can choose how I express this"*, or *"I am safe to speak my truth."* In this state, the Higher Self is available, and your thoughts reflect clarity and choice.

However, when the body moves into fight-or-flight mode, your inner voice changes quickly. It becomes urgent, defensive, protective: *"I have to defend myself." "They're going to hurt me." "I must control this."* These are not neutral thoughts. They are fear-driven messages shaped by the body's survival response.

And when you enter **freeze**, the internal dialogue often collapses into helplessness or shame: *"It's pointless." "I shouldn't speak." "I'm too much, better to stay quiet."* This is not a conscious choice. The nervous system attempts to keep you safe by withdrawing.

This is why paying attention to your inner dialogue is so important. The thoughts you hear in your mind are not random. They are direct reflections of your body's state. And when you learn to recognise them, you begin to understand when you are no longer in your Adult Self, and how to return.

The more you witness these shifts with compassion, the more freedom you will have to choose your words, tone, and truth, from soul, not from survival.

HOW SAFETY OR SURVIVAL SHAPES WHAT YOU SAY

*When you stop believing your reactive voice,
you start reclaiming your true one.*

Your nervous system acts as a kind of **"gatekeeper"** for your inner voices. Depending on whether you feel safe or under threat, different parts of you will take the lead. In moments of calm, your Adult Self can rise and guide your words with the assistance of your Higher Self. However, when your body senses danger, real or imagined, your protective parts often rush forward instead. In sympathetic arousal, the Inner Child or Inner Parent voices may dominate; in dorsal collapse, the Adult Self may be silenced altogether.

Understanding this dynamic is key to transforming how you communicate. You cannot force your Higher Self to lead when your body is locked in a state of survival response. But you can learn to recognise these shifts, and create enough safety in the system for your Higher Self to become available again.

When the Inner Child leads, words are often impulsive or overly emotional. When the Inner Parent dominates, the tone becomes rigid, cold, or shaming. When the Adult Self manages, speech may become overly cautious or performative.

Here's how different nervous system states "gate" which voices are likely to speak:

In a calm (ventral vagal) state:

- Your Higher Self is accessible
- Your Adult Self can choose words intentionally
- Your tone is softer, open, and connected to your heart
- Words are slower, more reflective, and less defensive.

You can listen deeply, express clearly, and hold compassion for yourself and others.

In a sympathetic (fight/flight) state:

- The Inner Child voice often dominates; reactive, fearful, urgent
- The Inner Parent can also get louder, criticising or controlling to "keep you safe"
- Tone becomes sharper, louder, faster, or more urgent
- Words may be aggressive, blaming, defensive, designed to protect or overpower
- The drive is to "fix it" quickly, or to escape.

In a dorsal vagal (freeze/collapse) state:

- The voice may disappear; going silent or shutting down
- The Inner Child may become helpless, hopeless, or withdrawn
- Speech may sound soft, flat, or disembodied
- Words may not come easily, or may be apologetic, disengaged, or disconnected from genuine feeling
- You may struggle to find words at all or feel emotionally numb.

The more you learn to recognise these patterns, not as flaws, but as survival responses, the more choice you will have.

When you can say to yourself: *"Ah, my system is in fight right now. That's why my tone is sharp"* or *"I notice I've gone into freeze. No wonder I can't find my words"* — you are already building the capacity to return to your Higher Self more quickly.

This is one of the great turning points on the path of conscious communication: when you stop believing your reactive voices and start understanding the state beneath them.

And as you begin to hear these shifts in your voice, in tone, in pace, in energy, you will start to catch, in real time, when your body is speaking from survival, and when you are ready to return to your truth.

DISTORTED EMOTIONS = DISTORTED COMMUNICATION

> *Distorted emotions are one of the most evident signs that your voice is no longer speaking from the present, but from the past.*

When your nervous system is dysregulated, locked in survival mode, it is not just your tone and pace that change. Your emotions themselves become distorted. And distorted emotions almost always lead to **distorted communication.**

You may have noticed this in your own life: when you are calm, you can express emotions clearly and cleanly, without blame, without collapse, without defence. But when you are under stress, when old triggers have been activated, the feelings you feel are often exaggerated, reactive, or tangled with old wounds. And these emotions then distort your words.

For example:

1. **Distorted anger** may come out as blame: *"You never listen!"*
2. **Distorted fear** may sound like avoidance: *"Oh, it's fine... it doesn't matter."*

3. **Distorted sadness** may collapse into helplessness: *"No one ever cares what I think."*

When you are in a regulated state, natural emotion flows differently:

- *"I feel unheard when this happens. Can we talk about it?"*
- *"I feel anxious about this decision. I'd like to slow down and think it through."*
- *"I'm feeling sad today. I just need a little space."*

This is why learning to recognise distorted emotions is so important. **It is one of the clearest signals that your system is dysregulated, and that you are speaking from survival, not from your Adult and Higher Self.**

As you build this awareness, you can begin to pause and ask: *"Is what I'm about to say coming from a clear emotion? Or from an old, distorted pattern?"* With practice, this one question can transform the way you communicate with yourself and with others.

WORDS, TONE, AND PACE - THE BODY'S TELLS

Your tone, your pace, your words, all reveal the state of your nervous system.

When your nervous system is activated, your body sends unmistakable signals, and these signals shape your communication more than you may realise. **Your voice, tone, and pace are among the first places where this shows up.**

For example, distorted anger might come out as blame: *"You never listen!"*

Distorted fear might come out as avoidance: *"Oh, it's fine, it doesn't matter."*

Natural emotion allows: *"I feel unheard when this happens. Can we talk about it?"*

In a **fight state**, you may notice your voice speeds up, the body preparing to defend. Your tone may become sharper, more clipped, or confrontational. Sentences may shorten, words becoming abrupt or even cutting. The volume may rise unconsciously, and your speech may feel pressured, driven by adrenaline rather than intention.

In a **flight state**, you may find yourself talking too much, over-explaining, justifying, trying to appease or smooth over discomfort. Sentences may run on, tone may sound nervous or forced, and words may tumble out faster than you intended.

In a **freeze state**, the opposite happens: your voice may soften, flatten, or even disappear. Words become sparse, hesitant, or swallowed. You may find it hard to access the words you want. A kind of mental blankness as the body shuts down. Even your rhythm and inflection can become subdued, as your system retreats from perceived threat.

These are the "tells" of your body's state, expressed through voice. And as you begin to notice these shifts in real time, you gain one of the most potent tools for conscious growth. You start to hear when you speak from a place of survival, rather than your soul. This is not something to judge, but to witness, with compassion. Because the moment you notice… You are already returning to presence. And from there, you can choose again.

CALMING YOUR SYSTEM TO HEAR YOUR SOUL

*You are not stuck with your old programming.
Safety is the doorway. From there, your
authentic voice can emerge.*

Your Higher Self is always present, not something you need to find or create, but when your body is in survival mode, its voice is often drowned out by the noise of protective parts. If your nervous system is braced in fight or flight, or collapsed in freeze, the mind narrows, focusing on protection rather than connection. In this state, your Higher Self cannot lead.

The first step is not about forcing positivity or controlling the mind, it is about calming the body. You create the inner conditions where the Higher Self can be heard by helping the nervous system feel safe. The goal is not to "erase" all stress, but to remind your system: *"I am safe enough, in this moment, to open. I can choose my words from love, not fear."*

Breath, grounding, and body-based tools are some of the most effective ways to do this. Slow, conscious breathing signals the nervous system to release tension. Grounding through the feet, sensory awareness, soothing touch all bring the body back to the here and now. Gentle movement, humming, or therapeutic shaking helps discharge stuck survival energy. These simple tools retrain the nervous system toward flexibility, rather than chronic defence.

For more profound or more persistent dysregulation, especially when there is trauma or long-term stress, additional supports may be needed. Neuroscience-based rewiring, somatic therapy, such as TRE (Tension and Trauma Releasing Exercises), Somatic Experiencing, and EMDR, can help process stored patterns. Polyvagal-informed practices; like singing, chanting, vagal massage, stimulate the vagus nerve and build safety in the body.

For some individuals, particularly those experiencing **depression, trauma symptoms, or nervous system "collapse"**, clinical tools may also play an important role. **Medications such as antidepressants or anxiolytics (under medical supervision)** can help stabilise an overwhelmed system, providing the safety needed for deeper emotional and spiritual work to unfold. Other options, such as neuroscience-based rewiring, neurofeedback or vagal nerve stimulation, are also tranformational for those with long-standing nervous system rigidity.

There is no shame in using any tool that helps. **What matters is restoring your capacity to hear your soul, allowing your authentic voice to** emerge, and no longer continuing to mask it.

The more you work with your body and your mind together, the more available your Higher Self becomes. You are teaching your system that safety is possible. That healing is possible. That you can trust yourself again.

And here is where **neuroscience-based rewiring offers extraordinary hope and speed**. Because your brain is not fixed. It is changeable, adaptable, and capable of profound transformation. Every emotion, belief, and reactive pattern is wired into your neural pathways, and with the right processes, these patterns can be shifted much faster than through slow repetition or talk alone. And here is where neuroscience offers us even greater hope: **your brain is not fixed, it can be rewired**. Through conscious practices, new emotional experiences, repetition, and compassion, you can reshape your inner pathways. The old limiting beliefs and emotional patterns stored in the subconscious can be released, not just intellectually, but in your body and nervous system.

Every time you choose breath over reaction… presence over defence… compassion over criticism… You are laying new neural pathways. Every time you speak from your Adult Self with the guidance of your Higher Self, you are reprogramming the mind toward truth.

When you work with a practitioner trained in neuroscience-based rewiring methods, someone who understands how to access and change the subconscious patterns at the root of your survival responses, you can rewire old beliefs and emotions at the source **quickly and efficiently**. This is not about years of analysis or slow behavioural change. It is about directly updating the body-mind system, so you no longer have to fight your old programming.

Every time you engage in this kind of neuroplastic work, releasing stuck emotions, clearing limiting beliefs, integrating new truths, you are creating new neural pathways that align with your soul's voice. You are removing the layers that once blocked your Higher Self, allowing it to guide your words, actions, and life.

And when this work is supported by body-based practices, therapy, or medical support where needed, the change is even more profound, because it is integrated at every level: physical, mental, emotional, and spiritual.

In the following pages, we will explore simple practices that can support this process and why working with the right tools and the right practitioner can accelerate your return to your authentic self.

CLEARING SURVIVAL PATTERNS: TOOLS FOR REWIRING THE BODY AND MIND

> *There is no one right way. Only what helps your system feel safe enough to change.*

There is no single path to healing. No one "right way." Each person's nervous system is unique, shaped by their history, their body, and their experiences. What matters is finding the approaches that support your system in feeling safe, open, and ready to receive new possibilities. The more safety you create in your body and mind, the more accessible your Higher Self becomes. And as the old survival patterns begin to dissolve, your voice will naturally shift, no longer speaking from defence, but from your truth. The practices that follow, both neuroscience-based and holistic, can all support this return to authentic voice and soul-guided communication.

Neuroscience-based Change (Fastest for Rewiring Patterns)

Neuroscience-based belief and emotional clearing rewiring protocols

- Practitioner-led processes that directly update subconscious

neural pathways
- Faster change than talk alone, clears survival patterns at the root
- Releases the need to fight old programming
- Changing survival reflexes and subconscious emotional loops
- Repatterning core beliefs about safety, worth, love, and belonging.

EMDR (Eye Movement Desensitisation & Reprocessing)
- Powerful for trauma-based patterns and emotional charge
- Neurofeedback
- Rewires brain-wave patterns for stability, regulation, and flexibility.

Vagal nerve stimulation / polyvagal-informed protocols
- Builds nervous system resilience
- Creates "neuro-permission" for the Higher Self to come forward.

Body-based & Somatic Practices

TRE (Tension & Trauma Releasing Exercises)
- Releases stored survival energy from the body
- Frees the nervous system from chronic fight/flight/freeze.

Somatic Experiencing (Peter Levine)
- Gradual trauma resolution through body awareness.

Feldenkrais Method, Qi Gong, Tai Chi
- Builds nervous system flexibility through gentle movement.

Therapeutic yoga (not fitness-based)

- Resets the breath-body connection
- Enhances vagal tone and sense of safety.

Breathwork

- Diaphragmatic, box breathing, heart-focused coherence somatic breathwork.

Healing

- Spinal Flow technique
- Reiki healing.

Simple Daily Practices to Support Regulation

- Grounding through feet, nature, or touch
- Self-soothing touch: hand on heart, gentle face touch
- Humming, chanting, singing (stimulates vagus nerve)
- Weighted blanket or warm bath
- Slow walks in nature
- Heart-focused meditation or compassion meditation.

Medical & Clinical Support When Needed

Antidepressants or anxiolytics (with medical guidance)

- Can stabilise an overwhelmed system, especially when frozen or collapsed
- Creates the space for deeper emotional and soul work to unfold.

Vagal nerve stimulation (clinical device)

- Used in treatment-resistant nervous system dysregulation.

Trauma-focused therapy
- Integrated approaches combining talk, body, and neuro-based work.

SPEAKING FROM A REGULATED STATE

So, how do we hear the Higher Self? How do we allow it to guide our words? The Higher Self speaks through the **Adult Self, the decision-making and observing part of your mind.** The part that can pause, reflect, and choose. But it cannot be heard clearly when the nervous system is dysregulated. When you are in fight, flight, or freeze, your body's survival reflexes take over, and the reactive voices of the Inner Child or Inner Parent rush forward, often hijacking your words and tone.

The Higher Self, by contrast, speaks with quiet clarity. It does not control or shame, it simply offers direction. You may have felt this before: that subtle voice during deep grief or overwhelm that says, *"Move your body." "Take a breath." "Reach out." "You'll be OK."* It is not forceful or loud, which is why it is so often missed beneath the noise of emotion. Yet it is the voice of alignment, the voice of your authentic self.

But to truly shift, you must also learn to listen: **Which voice is speaking right now?** Is it the Inner Child, trying to protect from old pain? The Inner Parent, criticising or controlling? Or the Adult making decisions and observing, while also receiving guidance from the Higher Self?

> *When the body feels safe, the mind regains choice, and the Higher Self can be heard.*

The gateway to mastering this is not perfection, it is awareness. You must become skilled at identifying the agendas of your inner voices: *Is this coming from old stories? From old wounds? From a learned survival pattern? Or is this the voice of growth, truth, and compassion?*

In the moment, this means learning to pause and ask: *Am I speaking from a regulated state? Is my breath steady, my tone open, my words chosen with care? Or am I reacting from dysregulation?* When you notice this, you can pause, using breath, grounding, and other body-based tools, and return to a calm state.

From this state, the Higher Self becomes available again. And with practice, you can learn to prepare for meaningful conversations by regulating first, creating the conditions for your soul's voice to lead, not your past pain.

NEUROSCIENCE-BASED CHANGE: THE FASTEST PATH TO REWIRING SURVIVAL PATTERNS

Change does not have to be slow. Your brain is wired for growth and transformation.

When it comes to releasing old emotional patterns and limiting beliefs, **neuroscience-based methods are among the most effective tools available.** Unlike approaches that rely solely on conscious thought, such as positive thinking, affirmations, or years of repetition. These methods work directly with the subconscious and the nervous system, where your survival patterns are truly stored.

Every negative belief, every reactive pattern you carry was formed through experience, and it became wired into the neural pathways of your brain and body. For example, a belief like *"I must not upset people"* often leads to soft, vague, or apologetic speech. When a belief is rewired and the Higher Self leads, the voice becomes clearer, more direct, and free from fear of rejection. The subconscious is not moved by logic or good intentions; it is moved by experience. And unless you change those pathways at the level where they were created, in the body, in the emotional memory, in the nervous system, the old patterns will continue to play out, no matter how much you "know better."

This is where neuroscience-based methods excel. They are designed to help you access these stored imprints. The places where old pain, fear, and unhelpful beliefs live, and to update them quickly. Unlike the slow path of simply repeating new thoughts and hoping for change, these processes work with how the brain learns: through emotional experience, neural plasticity, and the integration of new, safer pathways.

When used skilfully, these methods can bring about **almost immediate shifts** in perception, emotion, and behaviour. Clients often describe it as: *"The charge is gone." "I don't react the same way anymore." "It's like my body knows I'm safe now."*

Because the brain is constantly changing, reshaping itself with every experience. When you work at this level, you are not just managing symptoms; you are rewiring the core of the pattern. And this creates lasting change: in how you feel, think, speak, and ultimately, how you live.

This is the work I specialise in with clients: helping you release the outdated patterns held in the subconscious, so you can speak and live from your authentic self, not from your old pain. Neuroplasticity gives us a powerful truth: no matter how long you've been stuck in a pattern, change is always possible. And it can happen far faster than you may believe.

And while this kind of profound, neuroscience-based change rewires the core patterns, making authentic expression possible, you still need to know how to recognise what state you're in, moment by moment. Because even as the old patterns dissolve, life will still bring challenges. The nervous system can still be triggered. And in those moments, how you manage your state, how you return to calm, is what allows the voice of your Higher Self to lead. This is why speaking from a regulated state is so essential, and why building that skill in your daily life is one of the greatest gifts you can give yourself.

SIMPLE PRE-CONVERSATION PRACTICES TO REGULATE YOUR SYSTEM

Before entering a conversation that matters, especially one that may bring emotional charge, take a few minutes to centre yourself. These simple practices will help calm your nervous system, making space for your Higher Self to lead:

Breathwork: Slow, deep diaphragmatic breathing (inhale for 4, exhale for 6). Do 6–10 rounds to regulate the system.

Grounding through the body:

- Place both feet firmly on the floor
- Press palms into thighs or a table
- Focus on the feeling of contact with the earth. This signals "safety" to the body.

Soothing touch:

- Hand on heart or belly while breathing
- Self-hug or gentle stroking of arms, engages the calming parasympathetic system.

Simple vagus nerve stimulation:

- Hum softly for 1–2 minutes
- Sing or chant (even quietly)
- Stimulates the vagus nerve and brings calm.

Set a soul intention:

Before you begin, ask: *"What part of me do I want to lead this conversation?"*

- Choose: Higher Self, Adult Self, or old survival voice?

Permission to pause:

Permit yourself to pause during the conversation if needed, to breathe, to return to calm, to reconnect with your Higher Self or, at the very least, your Adult Self's voice of reason.

The more you practise regulating your nervous system, before conversations, during moments of stress, and in daily life, the more consistently your prefrontal cortex stays online. You regain access to choice, reflection, and intentional speech, rather than falling into automatic, reactive patterns. Over time, this reduces the dominance of old survival responses, allowing your communication to become more authentic and congruent.

~

You now understand how deeply your nervous system shapes not only what you feel, but also how you speak, how you think, and how you relate to others. You also now have tools to begin building regulation, to create the space where conscious choice is possible again. But nervous system patterns are only part of the picture. To truly shift old responses, we also need to explore the emotional triggers that keep pulling us back into reactivity, the unresolved patterns stored in our deeper mind that shape perception, meaning, and self-belief. In the next chapter, we will explore these emotional pathways and learn how to transform them from the inside out.

REFLECTION & INTEGRATION

Reflection Prompts for Speaking from a Regulated State

1. **Listening to My Body First**

   Daily Check-In

   - When did my body speak before my mind today?
   - What signs of stress or safety did I notice in my breath, posture,

or tone?

- How did that influence the way I communicated?

Alignment Intention: I commit to noticing: *"Where is this response starting? In my body or my mind?"*

2. **Mapping My Mind-Body Connection**

   Evening Reflection

   - When did my body feel stressed before I consciously knew why?
   - When did a thought or worry create tension in my body?
   - How did either shape the tone, words, or energy in my communication?

   Alignment Intention: *I will begin tracking how my body and mind interact, so I can shift with awareness.*

3. **Spotting My State in the Moment**

   Mini Pause Practice (2–3x/day)

   - What state am I in right now?

     (Safe → calm / Fight-flight → tense / Freeze → shut down)

   - What are the clues?

     (My breath? My tone? My body language?)

   - How is this affecting what I say? Or don't say?

   Alignment Intention: *I pause, name my state, and invite presence before I speak.*

4. **Listening to My Inner Voice**

   In Moments of Emotional Charge

   - What is the voice in my head saying right now?

- Is it calm, fearful, critical, or supportive?
- Is this my Higher Self, or a protective part?

Alignment Intention: *I notice the voice and choose whether to follow it.*

5. **Who Was Speaking for Me Today?**

   End-of-Day Check-In

   - In a key interaction, what state was I in (calm, anxious, shut down)?
   - Who was leading? Inner Child, Inner Parent, Adult Self or Higher Self?
   - What helped me notice this? (Tone, thoughts, breath?)
   - What could I try next time to shift faster into alignment?

   Alignment Intention: *I reflect without judgment, and choose more consciously next time.*

6. **Am I Speaking from Distortion or Clarity?**

   Before a Conversation

   - What emotion am I bringing in?
   - Is this a natural, present-moment emotion, or a distortion from an old belief?
   - How might this shape my tone, expression, or presence?

   Alignment Intention: I pause and ask: *"Is this my truth? Or my old survival strategy?"*

7. **How Is My Body Speaking Through My Voice?**

   After a Conversation or a Trigger

   - How did my tone, pace, or presence feel?
   - Did I speak from calm or anxiety, shutdown, or people-pleasing?

- What felt aligned and what didn't?

Alignment Intention: *I use my voice as a mirror and adjust with self-compassion.*

8. **How Am I Supporting My Change?**

Self-Support Check-In

- What practices (breathwork, grounding, movement) help me stay calm?
- Where could I use more support (e.g., somatic work, belief clearing, facilitation)?
- What would it feel like to allow myself to be helped truly?

Alignment Intention: *I deserve support. I allow myself what helps me grow.*

9. **Choosing My Tools for Change**

Empowered Planning

- What tools have helped me shift my voice, triggers, or stress response?
- Which ones could I deepen or return to now?
- Where could I ask for guidance or co-regulation?

Alignment Intention: *I utilise every tool available to help me reconnect with my true self.*

10. **Which Voice Is Leading Me?**

Real-Time Awareness Practice

- What state is my body in right now?
- Who is speaking? Inner Child, Inner Parent, Adult Self, or Higher Self?
- Am I responding from love, fear, or habit?

Alignment Intention: *I choose my speaker with care, presence, and truth.*

11. Preparing My Voice for Change

Voice Repatterning Reflection

- What beliefs are still shaping my tone or presence?
- Where am I ready to let go of survival-based patterns?
- What simple practice can help me stay regulated and congruent today?

Alignment Intention: *My voice is allowed to reflect the truth I now live.*

12. What's This Emotion Telling Me?

Trigger Inquiry Practice

- Is this a natural, clear emotion, or a distorted emotion from the past?
- What belief, memory, or expectation is this emotion referencing?
- What would my Higher Self want me to know right now?

13. Journal Prompt - Emotional Pattern Mapping

Think of one emotional reaction this week that surprised or overwhelmed you.

Write:

- What happened?
- What did I feel in my body?
- What belief was driving this?
- What would a natural response have looked like?
- What truth is my Higher Self inviting me into?

14. Realignment Practice - Distorted vs. Natural Emotion

Choose one recurring emotional pattern (e.g., anxiety, anger, avoidance). For 3 days:

Each time it surfaces, pause and ask:

- "Is this from now or from the past?"
- "What belief or fear is being triggered?"
- "What new truth could I try instead?"

Alignment Intention: One pause. One breath. One realignment at a time.

7

DECODING EMOTIONAL TRIGGERS: PATHWAYS TO HEALING

Emotional triggers are not random. They are patterns, built from past experiences, stored in the nervous system, and reinforced by the mind over time. Every time you feel a strong, disproportionate emotional response to a situation, it is a signal: an old wound has been touched. And until these triggers are recognised and processed, they will continue to shape not only how you feel, but how you speak, act, and experience yourself.

> *Triggers are not about the present moment. They are echoes of the past, asking to be healed.*

Some triggers even grow stronger over time, through emotional layering, where unprocessed wounds pile up, creating heightened reactivity. And in those moments, the old voices of your Inner Child or Inner Parent can easily hijack your words and tone.

In this chapter, we will explore how emotional triggers form, how they drive reactivity, and how you can begin to unhook from them, so your present-moment communication can reflect who you are now, not who you had to be to survive in the past.

WHAT ARE TRIGGERS - AND WHY DO THEY HIJACK US?

A trigger is not simply an emotional reaction, it is a **survival response** activated by an **unhealed emotional imprint**. At its core, a trigger is the body and nervous system reacting to a perceived threat that mirrors a past wound. Your brain is wired for survival: when it senses danger, it acts before you think. If an experience in the present, a word, a tone, a look, a situation, feels similar to an old emotional injury, your nervous system fires off a survival reflex: fight, flight, or freeze.

In that moment, it fires within a split second, where your rational Adult Self is no longer in charge. You are in an automatic response based on your old patterns, beliefs and unresolved emotions. You are no longer responding to *this person, this moment*. You are reacting to *that past experience*, often without even knowing it. This is why triggers hijack us: **they bypass conscious choice**. They pull us into automatic patterns designed to protect us, even when those patterns no longer serve who we are now.

Understanding this is key because once you can recognise a trigger for what it is, you can begin to change how you respond. You can start to reclaim your words, your tone, your presence, and move from reaction to choice.

HOW TRIGGERS ARE FORMED: THE EMOTIONAL BLUEPRINT OF THE PAST

Triggers are created through lived experience, typically long before we develop the ability to process emotions consciously. In childhood, when the brain is still developing, any experience that feels overwhelming, shaming, unsafe, or rejecting can leave a lasting emotional imprint. Suppose there was no opportunity to process or resolve those feelings at the time. In that case, the nervous system stores the event as a survival memory because it lacks the full capacity in the prefrontal cortex or if unresolved issues aren't dealt with or supported.

Over time, your mind builds beliefs around these unprocessed experiences: *"I must not upset people." "I'm too much." "It's not safe to express myself."* These beliefs, paired with stored emotion in the body, create **emotional blueprints** that shape how you experience future events. And because your subconscious is constantly scanning for threat, when a present moment resembles that old experience, even slightly, the blueprint fires.

The nervous system doesn't know it's reacting to the past. It responds as if the threat is happening *now*. This is why you can feel flooded, defensive, anxious, or shut down in situations that seem minor to others. You are not reacting to *this moment*, you are responding to the **pattern** created by your emotional history.

WHEN THE PAST HIJACKS THE PRESENT: HOW TRIGGERS DISTORT CONVERSATIONS

One of the most challenging aspects of being human is that in the moments when we most want to speak clearly; to express how we feel, to connect, and to resolve, old triggers can hijack us. And when this happens, we are no longer responding to the current moment with fresh perception. We are speaking through layers of experience.

> *When you're triggered, you're not responding to this person, you're responding to years of layers.*

This is **emotional layering** in action. Every unhealed wound, every unprocessed emotion, adds a new layer to your inner blueprint. And when a present moment touches that old pain, even slightly, the entire stack of unresolved emotion can activate at once. This is why some reactions feel so disproportionate: *you're not responding to this person. You're responding to years of layers.*

In conversations, this can sound like:

- **Blame or attack:** *"You never listen!"* — when the current issue was minor, but the old wounds of feeling unheard were deep
- **Collapse or withdrawal:** *"It's fine, it doesn't matter."* — when the real feeling is sadness or fear, but past experiences taught you it wasn't safe to speak
- **Over-explaining or fawning:** *"I just wanted to make sure you're okay with this. Is that okay?"* — when old rejection wounds drive people-pleasing.

In these moments, your body is signalling "this is unsafe", even if the current situation is not dangerous. And your words, tone, and presence will be shaped by that state. You may find yourself thinking later: *"Why did I react like that?"*, not realising that it was the **layers**, not the present, that were speaking through you.

Recognising this is powerful because when you can feel the difference between an authentic response and a layered trigger reaction, you regain choice. You can pause, ground yourself, and decide: *"Do I want to speak from this old pattern or from who I am now?"*

REWIRING TRIGGERS: FREEING YOUR VOICE FOR AUTHENTIC EXPRESSION

Emotional triggers don't disappear through avoidance or control, they transform through conscious recognition, regulation, and reprocessing. Rewiring your emotional triggers isn't about becoming "unbothered" or always calm. It's about returning faster to truth and choosing your voice rather than reacting from old pain.

This is the work of becoming emotionally congruent: where your tone, your pace, your language, and your presence reflect the you that exists now, not the wounded version from your past.

Let's explore the steps that make this possible:

1. Interrupting the Trigger-Response Cycle

The first step in rewiring a trigger is recognising when it's happening.

A trigger response often begins in the body, a tightening in the chest, heat in the face, a lump in the throat, a flood of thoughts, or a sudden urge to shut down or lash out. These are your cues.

To interrupt the cycle:

- **Pause before reacting.** A five-second pause is often enough to re-engage the prefrontal cortex
- **Name what's happening.** Say to yourself, *"I'm triggered right now. This isn't just about what's in front of me."*
- **Orient to the present.** Use grounding statements like: *"I am here. This is now. I am safe."*

Disrupting the automatic reaction creates a tiny window where choice becomes possible. And over time, this window becomes wider.

2. Returning to the Adult Self + Higher Self Voice

Once you've paused, your goal is to return to the part of you that can respond from clarity: your **Adult Self** and **Higher Self**.

These voices do not panic. They don't need to defend, withdraw, or attack. They are rooted in the present, in wisdom and compassion.

To return to them:

- Place a hand on your heart or belly. This reconnects you to your body and anchors your awareness
- Ask: *"What part of me is feeling activated right now?"* Is it the

Inner Child (abandoned, rejected)? The Inner Parent (critical, shaming)?
- Then ask: *"What would my rational Adult Self say?" "What would my Higher Self offer in this moment?"*

These questions don't deny the trigger. They bring guidance to it.

3. Rewiring Triggers Through Neuroscience + Awareness

The brain doesn't rewire through information alone. It needs new experiences of safety paired with new emotional meanings.

This is how emotional memory is reconsolidated:

- **Feel the trigger.** Stay present with the emotion without getting lost in it
- **Introduce new meaning.** While staying regulated, gently reframe the old belief *("I'm not safe," "I'm too much")* with a soul-aligned truth: *"This is a reminder from the past, but I'm not in that time anymore."*
- **Reinforce safety through the body.** Breathe, ground, use self-touch, or move slowly. Letting your body feel what it's like to stay present with the discomfort and not abandon yourself.

Every time you experience a trigger differently, your brain updates the associated neural pathway, dissolving the charge and embedding new emotional safety.

Neuroscience-based change techniques, such as emotional memory reconsolidation, bilateral stimulation, and pattern interruption, can accelerate this rewiring process, primarily when facilitated by a trained practitioner.

4. Healing Triggers to Restore Congruence

When triggers no longer hijack your voice, something powerful happens: you become congruent.

Congruence means:

- You say what you mean, without distortion
- Your tone matches your intention
- Your emotions guide you, not control you
- You are clear, calm, and grounded, even in challenging conversations.

This doesn't mean you never feel upset. It means your **response is no longer shaped by fear or conditioning**, but by presence and self-leadership.

Your voice becomes a reflection of your healing.

This is what rewiring offers: not perfection, but integration. Not silence, but self-trust. A voice that speaks from now, not from then.

~

Now that you've seen how your nervous system shapes your emotional responses and communication, we go deeper into the hidden forces at play. The old beliefs and unconscious programming that hijack your voice in real time. This chapter reveals how the past doesn't just live in memory; it speaks through you, often without your permission. And more importantly, how to change that.

Later, you'll learn what happens when this outdated Inner Parent finally collapses, and why that breakdown IS your breakthrough.

REFLECTION & INTEGRATION

Becoming conscious of your triggers doesn't start with changing how you feel. It starts with observing when and where the emotional charge takes over. This is the practice of self-awareness in real time: not to shame or fix, but to learn, soften, and rewire.

Below are guided prompts and practices to help you begin recognising where your past may be shaping your present, especially in your communication.

Awareness Practice: "Where Did I React from a Layer?"

At the end of the day or week, reflect on your interactions:

- Where did I overreact to something small?
- Where did I shut down, retreat, or become defensive without fully understanding why?
- Was my response actually about the current person or moment... or was it about something deeper inside me?

Use this guiding sentence:

> *"I wasn't reacting to the person in front of me. I was reacting to the layer of _____ inside me."*

Examples:

- *"...the rejection I felt in childhood."*
- *"...my belief that I'm not good enough."*
- *"...my fear that I'll be abandoned."*

Let the insight come without judgment. You're not wrong for reacting. You're just meeting yourself more clearly now.

Real-Time Trigger Spotting Exercise

In your next few conversations, especially the emotionally charged or uncomfortable ones:

1. **Pause for 3 to 5 seconds before speaking.**
   - This gives your nervous system a moment to stabilise
   - Ask silently: *"Is this my true voice, or a reaction from the past?"*
2. **Observe your body:**
   - Is there heat, tightness, clenching, or shallow breathing?

- Is your tone sharper, louder, flatter, or overly sweet?

3. **Spot the voice:**
    - Is this my Inner Child trying to be heard?
    - Is this my Inner Parent trying to control?
    - Is my Adult Self or Higher Self online right now?

4. **Optional reframe (silently or aloud):**
    - "What I really need right now is…"
    - "I'm feeling something deeper than just this moment."
    - "Let me pause. I want to respond with more clarity."

Journal Reflection Prompts:

Use these as daily or weekly journaling anchors:

- What conversation challenged me most this week?
- What part of me was leading that conversation? Inner Child, Inner Parent, Adult Self?
- What emotional or physical signs told me I was triggered?
- What was I *really* afraid of in that moment?
- What would my Higher Self have said or done differently?

Alignment Intention:

"I commit to recognising when the past is speaking through me and choosing presence instead of pattern."

You may not catch every trigger in the moment, and that's okay. Every time you reflect on an experience after the fact, you build your capacity to respond differently next time. That is healing. That is rewiring.

Part III

Rewire, Release & Realign

Where the old patterns fall away and your new voice begins.

Change doesn't happen from the neck up. It happens through integration. In this part, you'll learn how to shift what's been running you, from subconscious beliefs and emotional charges to outdated nervous system loops. Through neuroscience, emotional resolution, and soul guidance, you'll discover what rewiring truly looks like. This is where you stop trying to "think" your way free and start becoming who you really are.

8

WHEN THE PAST SPEAKS THROUGH YOU: WHY OLD PROGRAMS DISTORT VOICE, TONE, AND PRESENCE

Have you ever walked away from a conversation and thought to yourself, *"Why did I say that?"* or *"That didn't sound like me"*? You may have felt a pang of regret or confusion, wondering where that reaction or tone came from. It can be easy to dismiss it as a momentary lapse or a bad day, but these moments are rarely random. More often, they are signals: subtle indicators that something deeper was at play. What spoke in that moment was not your conscious, present-day self. It was an old survival program, an emotional imprint from the past, rising up and temporarily taking the lead.

Your voice is not just sound. It is an expression of your entire internal system: your emotional state, your belief system, your nervous system, and the energetic blueprint you carry in your body. When you speak, you're not only delivering words, you are communicating your history, your pain, your resilience, and your subconscious conditioning. The tone you use, the way your body holds itself, the speed of your speech, and even the silence between your words all hold meaning. They reflect not just what you think in the moment, but what you've lived. Especially if you have lived through experiences where speaking your truth felt dangerous, where being seen brought punishment, or where emotional expression led to rejection.

This is why **voice distortion** is one of the most evident signs of unresolved inner programming. You might say all the "right" things, even rehearsed ones, But if your tone is cold, anxious, overcompensating, apologetic, or defensive, others will feel the disconnect. And so will you. You'll sense it as an internal misalignment. A moment when something inside you knows: *"That wasn't my real voice. That was my fear speaking. That was a reflex, not a choice."*

When old beliefs are still active in the subconscious, beliefs like *"I'm too much," "I'm not enough," "I'll be rejected,"* or *"I have to perform to be loved"*. They don't just influence what you say. They determine how you say it. These beliefs shape your tone, pauses, posture, and presence. They cause you to shrink back when you need to speak up, to speak too much when you're afraid of silence, or to contort your truth to keep others comfortable. And perhaps most heartbreakingly, they can mute the voice of your Higher Self, the wise, grounded part of you that knows exactly how to speak with clarity and compassion.

But the reverse is also true.

When your inner world is congruent, when your beliefs are aligned with your inherent worth, when you feel emotionally safe, when your nervous system is regulated, your voice naturally reflects that. You speak more calmly. You listen more deeply. You choose your words from a place of presence, not panic. You don't need to perform or protect, you express. Your tone becomes congruent with your message, and people can feel the integrity of what you're saying because it's anchored in authenticity.

However, when your beliefs are still running on old scripts, shaped by childhood dynamics, trauma, abandonment, or fear of rejection, your voice and presence will mirror that. These subconscious programs distort your expression by hijacking your natural rhythm. They inject your tone with urgency, your sentences with justification, or your silence with shame. And while you may be doing your best to show up as a leader, friend, or partner, the part of you speaking may still be a child, trying to stay safe.

This is why communication isn't just about learning the "right" words or scripts. It's about **clearing the distortions** that live beneath your voice. Because when the past speaks for you, your present becomes unclear. Your leadership falters. Your relationships strain. And your sense of self becomes tangled with old roles and outdated truths.

Here's what that can look like in real time:

Subconscious Belief	How It Distorts Voice, Tone and Presence
"I have to prove myself to be worthy."	Over-explaining, justifying, and over-talking to avoid judgment.
"It's not safe to be seen."	Quiet voice, avoidance of eye contact, shrinking body posture.
"I'm not good enough."	Apologetic tone, downward inflection, filler words like "just" or "sorry."
"Others always reject me."	Defensive tone, pre-emptive withdrawal, rushing to speak or shutting down.
"I'll be punished if I speak honestly."	Careful, flat, or robotic tone, performing instead of expressing.

Subconscious Belief	How It Distorts Voice, Tone and Presence
"If I show emotion, I'll be weak."	Hyper-controlled voice, minimal facial expression, harsh tone.
"Love has to be earned."	Pleasing tone, prioritising harmony over truth, suppressing needs.

WHY THIS MATTERS FOR LEADERSHIP AND LIFE

In both personal and professional life, your voice is your power. When old beliefs distort your expression, you are no longer leading with your present self. You are leading with your past pain.

This creates what we call **leadership distortion:**

A dynamic where people either under-express (become overly passive, agreeable, or avoidant) or over-express (become controlling, harsh, or defensive), all because subconscious survival patterns are shaping their inner voices.

If your voice is distorted, people may hear fear instead of clarity, control instead of confidence, or performance instead of presence.

And the result?

You stay unseen.

You feel unheard.

You lose trust in your ability to express your truth, and others feel it, even if they can't name it.

But this doesn't have to be permanent. When you begin to notice the beliefs driving your words, and gently update those beliefs, your voice shifts naturally, not just in tone, but in confidence, congruence, and emotional resonance. But these distortions don't just live in your thoughts. They live in your body.

Even if your mind is trying to stay present, your tone, posture, and pacing may reveal something much older: a belief ingrained in your nervous system, shaped by past experiences. That's because beliefs are not just mental, they are embodied.

EMBODIED BELIEFS: WHY YOUR VOICE REVEALS WHAT YOU BELIEVE

We often think of beliefs as silent thoughts, phrases that run through the mind like background noise. However, the truth is that beliefs are not just mental. They are *fully embodied*. They live in your voice, your posture, your nervous system, your breath, and even in your silences.

Every time you speak, your body speaks with you. And that body is shaped by every belief you carry, especially the unconscious ones formed in moments of fear, vulnerability, or emotional imprinting.

If you hold the belief, "*I don't matter,*" it may not come out in words, but in hesitation. A drop in volume. A tightening in your chest. Shoulders that round inward. A voice that doesn't quite land.

If the belief is "*I need to be perfect,*" it may show up as a polished, overly rehearsed tone; speech that is fast, clipped, or strained. You might over-prepare or micromanage every word. Your body may sit rigidly; your breath held just under the surface.

Even silence carries belief. The moment you choose not to speak, when you bite your tongue, sugarcoat the truth, or avoid being seen, your body is expressing something:

> "*It's not safe to be honest.*"
> "*I'll be judged if I show too much.*"
> "*My needs don't matter.*"

These are not simply cognitive beliefs. They are *felt experiences*. And this is why mindset work alone often falls short. You can affirm *"I am enough"* a hundred times, but if your tone is apologetic, your voice quivers, and your body is braced, the belief hasn't changed.

The subconscious doesn't learn through logi. It learns through experience. *Through the body*. Through safety.

This is why belief work is also voice work. It's body work. It's nervous system work. To truly rewire a belief, you must change the *state* in which it lives.

That means:

- Regulating the nervous system
- Practising new emotional responses in real time
- Noticing the cues; your breath, your posture, your tone
- Rewiring by choosing new words and tones *while in a regulated state*. Not just when you're calm, but in the very moments that used to trigger you.

When your beliefs begin to shift, so does your voice. You slow down. Not from fear, but from presence. Your words land. Your tone warms. Your message becomes more congruent. Because it's finally safe to express your truth.

The more you bring awareness to these patterns, the more you reclaim your real voice. Not the one shaped by survival, but the one that was always yours.

~

When you understand that your Adult Self is not just a mindset but a state of leadership, you begin to reclaim the ability to guide, not just survive.

REFLECTION & INTEGRATION

Reflection Prompt - "Who Spoke for Me?"

Think of a conversation this week where you walked away feeling off, regretful, or emotionally stirred.

Ask yourself:

- What did I say? How did I say it?
- Did my tone, volume, or body language reflect fear, pressure, or performance?
- Which belief might have been silently driving how I spoke?
- Was it my Higher Self, Inner Child, Inner Parent, or rational Adult Self speaking?

Trigger Trace Exercise - Belief to Voice Map

Complete this for one conversation where you felt your voice wasn't congruent like in the table below:

Situation	What I Said	How I Said it	What I Felt	Likely Subconscious Belief	What I Wish I'd Said Instead
Example: My partner questioned my plans	"It's fine, I'll figure it out."	Flat tone, quiet, looked away	Resentment, shutdown	"I'm too much if I have needs."	"I do have a plan, and I'd love your support."

Repeat for 1–2 recent conversations.

Somatic Check-In - Voice Awareness

Next time you speak, especially under pressure, pause and notice:

- What is my breath doing right now?
- How does my voice sound; fast, flat, tight, soft, hesitant?
- What does my body posture suggest I believe in this moment?

Then try this grounding alignment: Hand on heart. Breathe deep. Ask: *"Is this my survival voice or my true voice?"*

Alignment Intention - Shaping Your Voice from Truth

Choose a daily mantra for the week ahead. Let it become an anchor when your old voice starts to lead:

- *"I don't need to prove. I just need to speak from presence."*
- *"My tone matters more than my script."*
- *"My truth can be soft and still powerful."*
- *"I can speak with kindness, without shrinking or performing."*

Journal Prompt - Reclaiming My Real Voice

- What belief has most distorted my voice in the past?
- How did I learn to speak that way? Where did I pick it up?
- How would my voice sound if I were completely safe, calm, and aligned with truth?
- What would it feel like to speak with that voice today?

9

WHY MINDSET ALONE CAN'T CLEAR TRIGGERS

Understanding the voices of your mind, and the agenda each carries, is foundational to lasting emotional healing. Without this awareness, you may believe you're making rational, conscious choices, when in reality, your Inner Parent or Inner Child is driving your reactions. And when either of these parts is leading, especially when triggered, your communication, behaviour, and even your self-perception becomes distorted.

Many people turn to mindset work or traditional talk therapy to untangle this inner conflict. While both have value, especially in helping you recognise patterns and give language to your experience, they often fall short of creating deep, embodied change. Why? Because they mostly work at the level of **conscious thought**, while the emotional drivers behind your triggers live much deeper, in the body, the nervous system, and the **subconscious mind** where your Inner Child and Inner Parent reside.

When your inner world is ruled by conflicting agendas, the demanding, emotional Inner Child and the rigid, critical Inner Parent, no amount of surface-level reframing can resolve that tension. It's like trying to mediate a shouting match by thinking harder. Even as you try to reason your way forward, the emotional volume inside continues to rise. Without intervention, this "win/lose" dynamic between the Inner Child and Inner Parent creates escalating psychic tension, an unresolved internal war that pulls energy, focus, and peace away from your present life.

In this state, many people find themselves desperate for resolution but emotionally overwhelmed. You may not even know what you need, only that something inside feels unbearably tight. If the Inner Child is crying out for attention, connection, or rest, and the Inner Parent continues to deny it, or worse, condemns it, then the system becomes emotionally gridlocked. The longer this impasse remains, the more you'll feel stuck, lost, or volatile.

This is often the moment people reach for relief through alcohol, substances, distraction, or overwork. Not because they're lazy or undisciplined, but because the **inner conflict has become unbearable**. And still, the Inner Parent refuses to let go of control. It clings to its rigid worldview, shaped by outdated programming, and insists it can solve the problem alone.

But it can't. And it won't.

The irony of the Inner Parent is that, for all its arrogance and control, it is rooted in fear. It doesn't trust others, doesn't want feedback, and certainly doesn't want to admit that it might be wrong. So it isolates. It ruminates. It tightens its grip, refusing to look outside itself for help. When it fails to fix the problem through its own narrow lens, it doesn't surrender, it attacks. It turns inward, blaming you: *"You should know better." "What's wrong with you?" "You always screw this up."* The guilt spiral begins, and now the Inner Parent, instead of protecting you, has become a second aggressor.

Meanwhile, the Inner Child, starved for compassion and emotional safety either collapses in shame or rises in rebellion. You might find yourself snapping at people, isolating, indulging in escapism, or emotionally shutting down. These are not failures of willpower. They are symptoms of **internal misalignment.** The parts of you meant to collaborate are at war. And without an active Adult Self to mediate, no resolution is possible.

The presence of the Adult Self is what changes everything.

The Adult Self is the only part of your internal system capable of **neutral observation.** It doesn't take sides, it listens. It hears the fear beneath the Inner Parent's control. It recognises the longing beneath the Inner Child's outbursts. It steps in as a mediator, a translator, a guide. And most importantly, it seeks a win/win, not a win/lose between the Inner Parent and Inner Child.

But here's the challenge: when trauma, emotional overload, or past conditioning has silenced the Adult Self voice, it cannot lead. The Inner Child and Inner Parent dominate, and the system spirals. You end up reacting from pain, not presence. From protection, not truth.

Let's take an example:

Your Inner Child feels overwhelmed and emotionally trapped. It's had enough of being told to *"be good," "be quiet,"* or *"be perfect."* The Inner Parent, rather than listening, tightens the rules. *"You don't get to complain. You're lucky to even be here."* The Inner Child rebels, not out of spite, but out of desperation. You start binge-eating, procrastinating, numbing, or self-sabotaging. The Inner Parent responds with more shame, more rules, more guilt.

This is the chaos loop. The inner battle escalates, and your conscious Adult Self is nowhere to be found.

Each of these dynamics shows why high emotional awareness and mindset alone are not enough to create lasting change. The subconscious, emotional parts of you, especially the Inner Child, **do not respond to logic**. They respond to emotional connection, nervous system regulation, and safety. The Inner Parent, too, must be taught a new way of leading, one rooted in humility, not shame.

True change comes when both voices are heard, but neither are in charge.

When the Adult Self is strong and supported, and when Higher Self guidance is invited in, you begin to move toward balance. You can recognise when the Inner Child is crying out… without obeying its every impulse. You can hear the Inner Parent's warnings… without believing its shame. You become the **conscious chooser**, not the echo of your past conditioning.

And this is why working at the level of the nervous system, subconscious beliefs, and emotional integration is essential. Otherwise, the very parts you're trying to change will continue running the show, hidden behind a mask of self-control or positive thinking.

WHEN THE INNER CHILD OVERRIDES THE INNER PARENT

When the Inner Parent loses control or influence, and the Inner Child overrides the Inner Parent with it's emotional unmet needs, and hijacks cognitive control, it may look like this in real life behaviours:

1. **Emotional impulsivity wins over discipline:**
   - Inner Parent says: *"You should go to bed early."*
   - Inner Child says: *"I'm too anxious. I need to binge Netflix and scroll for hours."*

   Result: Chronic sleep loss, emotional burnout, shame the next day.

2. **Soothing wins over control:**
   - Inner Parent says: *"You've already had enough wine."*

- Inner Child says: *"Just one more glass. I feel so alone tonight."*

Result: Over-drinking to soothe emotional pain, followed by guilt.

3. **Avoidance wins over responsibility:**
   - Inner Parent says: *"You need to pay that bill or answer that email."*
   - Inner Child says: *"I can't deal with pressure. I just want to escape."*

Result: Procrastination, self-sabotage, anxiety spiral later.

4. **People-pleasing wins over boundary-setting:**
   - Inner Parent says: *"You know this person always drains you."*
   - Inner Child says: *"But if I say no, they might not love me anymore."*

Result: Over-giving, resentment, emotional collapse later.

5. **Addiction wins over structure:**
   - Inner Parent says: *"You promised to stop this pattern."*
   - Inner Child says: *"Just this once. I can't cope right now."*

Result: Looping addictive cycles (emotional eating, porn, gambling, etc.)

6. **Validation-seeking wins over truth:**
   - Inner Parent says: *"You don't need to prove yourself."*
   - Inner Child says: *"If I don't perform, they'll reject me."*

Result: Overworking, overachieving, emotional disconnection.

7. **Fantasy wins over grounded presence:**
   - Inner Parent says: *"Stay focused. You're avoiding reality."*
   - Inner Child says: *"Let me escape into daydreaming / romantic obsession / scrolling."*

Result: Delayed growth, disempowerment, self-blame.

WHEN THE INNER PARENT SILENCES OR CONTROLS THE INNER CHILD

When the Inner Parent dominates, it often mimics the **voices of early caregivers**, especially when they used fear, shame, or performance-based love. Instead of offering guidance, the Inner Parent voice becomes punitive, suppressing the natural needs of the Inner Child (emotion, rest, creativity, play).

Over time, this silencing leads to emotional rigidity, chronic stress, and the loss of authenticity. Here's some grounded examples of when the Inner Parent dominates and suppresses the Inner Child:

1. **Suppressing Playfulness or Joy:**
   - Inner Child wants: *"Let's dance, laugh, be silly."*
   - Inner Parent says: *"That's childish. Be serious. You'll look foolish."*

   Result: Suppression of joy, creativity, and spontaneity. Chronic self-judgment.

2. **Shaming Emotional Needs:**
   - Inner Child says: *"I feel sad. I need comfort."*
   - Inner Parent says: *"You're too sensitive. Toughen up. Don't cry."*

   Result: Emotional repression, numbness, difficulty accessing vulnerability.

3. **Pushing Through Exhaustion:**
   - Inner Child says: *"I'm tired. I need rest."*
   - Inner Parent says: *"Rest is for the weak. You haven't done enough."*

   Result: Burnout, disconnection from body, over-identification with productivity.

4. **Silencing the Voice:**

- Inner Child says: *"I want to speak up. I feel hurt."*
- Inner Parent says: *"Don't make a scene. Keep the peace. Stay quiet."*

Result: People-pleasing, throat chakra suppression, difficulty setting boundaries.

5. **Invalidating Curiosity or Dreams:**
   - Inner Child says: *"I want to try something new!"*
   - Inner Parent says: *"That's not practical. You'll fail. Grow up."*

   Result: Self-doubt, stuckness, unfulfilled potential.

6. **Shaming Needs for Connection:**
   - Inner Child says: *"I feel lonely. I want love."*
   - Inner Parent says: *"Don't be needy. You should be independent."*

   Result: Isolation, fear of intimacy, self-reliance at the cost of connection.

7. **Moral Policing and Perfectionism:**
   - Inner Child says: *"I made a mistake. I need reassurance."*
   - Inner Parent says: *"You're a failure. You should have known better."*

   Result: Shame spirals, fear of failure, inner criticism.

Dynamic	Inner Child Overrides Inner Parent (Inner Child-Led)	Inner Parent Silences Inner Child (Inner Parent-Led)
Emotional Need	"I feel lonely... so I'll chase connection or attention any way I can."	"I feel lonely... but I shouldn't need anyone. I'll stay quiet and deal with it alone."
Stress Response	Impulsive action: binge eating, outbursts, avoidance.	Emotional shutdown, pressure to perform or suppress feelings.
Self-Expression	Speaks without filter: reactive, defensive, dramatic.	Suppresses voice: stays silent to avoid judgment or conflict.
Desire for Joy or Play	Indulges in distraction, pleasure-seeking, or rebellion.	Labels fun as unproductive or immature; focuses only on duties.
Mistake or Failure	Blames others, deflects, or acts out to avoid shame.	Harsh inner criticism, guilt, perfectionism.
Seeking Comfort	Reaches for external soothing (e.g., scrolling, substances).	Judges self for needing help; insists on independence.
Personal Boundaries	Can't hold boundaries; seeks approval.	Rigid, self-sacrificing; ignores own needs to appear "good" or "in control."
Decision Making	Emotion-driven: *"I want it now!"*	Rule-driven: *"You must do what's right, even if it hurts."*
Belief Patterns	"If I don't get what I want, I'll fall apart or won't be loved."	"If I make a mistake or need others, I'm weak or not good enough."
Higher Self Access	Blocked by chaos or emotional overwhelm.	Blocked by rigid beliefs and control mechanisms.

"I KNOW BETTER – BUT I STILL REACT"

It can be incredibly frustrating to "know better" and still find yourself repeating the same old patterns. You've done the work, gained insight, even made conscious decisions about who you want to be, and yet, in the heat of the moment, you react in a way that doesn't align with your values or goals.

This isn't a failure of willpower. It's a sign that your logical mind may have decided to move forward, but your unconscious mind is still tethered to the past. In these moments, it's not your conscious self reacting. It's your survival self. More specifically, it's often the Inner Parent whose beliefs, rules, and fears are still driving your behaviour from beneath the surface.

When old survival programs haven't been updated, particularly those formed in childhood or under stress, they will override your logic every time. Why? Because the unconscious mind doesn't prioritise growth, it prioritises safety. And until that part of you feels emotionally safe, it will keep pulling you back into what's familiar, even if it's no longer helpful.

If you find yourself stuck in cycles of unwanted behaviour, snapping at others, shutting down, over-giving, avoiding conflict, or seeking validation, it's not because you're broken. These patterns were **learned**. And anything learned can be **unlearned**.

This is why it's essential to meet yourself with **compassion**. There is no shame in having inherited or absorbed these protective strategies. However, there comes a point where continuing to live from outdated programming becomes a form of **self-abandonment.** And while your conditioning may not be your fault, **your healing is your responsibility**.

You didn't choose the wounds, but you do get to decide how long they run the show.

Rewiring these patterns is not just about thinking differently. It's about updating the internal systems that still believe you need them. It's about identifying the voice that keeps reacting, and giving your Higher Self, your conscious Adult Self, the space to lead instead.

You can change. You can update the scripts. And you can finally live and lead from your truth, rather than your programming.

YOUR SURVIVAL REFLEX - THE SUBCONSCIOUS MIND, NERVOUS SYSTEM, AND EMOTIONAL MEMORY

Your survival reflex is not just a feeling, it's a full-body, full-system response governed by the subconscious mind, your nervous system, and your stored emotional memory. From birth, your neural pathways begin collecting data: experiences, emotional reactions, meanings, beliefs, and somatic reflexes and become a deeply ingrained blueprint for how your system protects you. And until those unconscious programs are brought into awareness and rewired, they will continue to run your life, often in ways that feel out of your control.

Your subconscious doesn't ask for your permission. It reacts based on memory. And unless you either (1) reprogram those neural pathways, or (2) learn to catch your emotions mid-flight and override them with conscious decision-making, your system will default to what it knows: survival.

That second option, pausing in the moment, feeling the emotion, and choosing a new response, is a learned art form. And it takes **deep practice.**

Here's what's happening in real time:

The very moment your survival reflex is triggered, often by a word, a tone, a glance, or a situation that reminds your body of past pain, your limbic system takes the wheel. Your amygdala scans for danger and hits the emergency button. Your rational brain, the prefrontal cortex, temporarily powers down. The thinking mind is put on hold. Your system doesn't want analysis. It wants protection.

This all happens in a split second. You didn't *decide* to react that way, your body did it for you. Until you update the unconscious patterns stored in your system, this reflex will continue to hijack your presence and voice.

Here's what that can look like in everyday life when the unconscious mind overrides the Adult Self:

1. **A colleague offers feedback, and you feel instantly defensive.**

    Triggered belief: *"I'm never good enough."*

    Reaction: You snap back or justify quickly before listening. The Inner Child fears being shamed, and the Inner Parent piles on with internal criticism.

2. **You don't get a response to a message, and feel rejected.**

    Triggered belief: *"People always leave me."*

    Reaction: You ruminate, withdraw, or send a second message in an anxious state. The Inner Child fears abandonment, and the Inner Parent criticises you for "being too much."

3. **You're asked to speak in a meeting, and your mind goes blank.**

    Triggered belief: *"I'll say something wrong and be judged."*

    Reaction: You freeze, fumble, or speak with shaky energy. The body enters a dorsal vagal shutdown while the Inner Child tries to disappear.

4. **A friend cancels plans, and you feel angry.**

Triggered belief: *"I don't matter to people."*

Reaction: You lash out, ignore them, or punish them silently. It's the Inner Child reacting from hurt, not the Adult Self considering the context.

5. **You make a small mistake at work, and spiral into shame.**

   Triggered belief: *"If I fail, I'll lose love or safety."*

   Reaction: You beat yourself up, over-apologise, or overwork to "make up for it." Inner Parent domination.

6. **Someone sets a boundary with you, and you feel instantly rejected.**

   Triggered belief: *"If they loved me, they wouldn't push me away."*

   Reaction: You argue, guilt-trip, or shut down emotionally. The Inner Child feels abandoned, and old fears override empathy.

7. **You're around confident people, and you shrink.**

   Triggered belief: *"I'm not as good as them."*

   Reaction: You underplay your voice, fawn, or over-praise them. The unconscious belief creates a submissive posture and tone.

8. **You're asked how you feel, and you say, *"I'm fine"* without checking.**

   Triggered belief: *"My emotions are too much."*

   Reaction: You disconnect from your body and emotion entirely. The Inner Parent suppresses the Inner Child's vulnerability.

9. **A partner is late, and you panic or accuse them.**

Triggered belief: *"People don't value me."*

Reaction: You send emotionally charged messages or pull away in silence. It's not the Adult Self speaking. It's the old wound running the show.

10. **You feel emotional in public, and immediately push it down.**

Triggered belief: *"I must always be in control."*

Reaction: You suppress tears, tighten your jaw, or shift into perfectionist energy. The Inner Parent suppresses the Inner Child's need for expression.

These are not personality flaws. They are survival patterns. And if they sound familiar, it means your system has done everything it can to keep you safe, often at the cost of your authenticity.

The good news? These patterns can be rewired.

By working with the subconscious, the nervous system, and emotional memory, through neuroscience-based practices, somatic awareness, and guidance from your Higher Self, you can begin to reclaim your responses. You can return to your choice.

You can shift from automatic to authentic.

HOW TO CATCH A TRIGGER IN MID-FLIGHT

Once you recognise that your triggers are survival reflexes, not character flaws, the next step is learning to *interrupt* the pattern before it runs the show.

You won't always catch it in time. But the more you practise, the more you'll notice the subtle shifts, the change in breath, the rise of tension, the sudden urge to defend, fix, justify, or disappear. These are the *early signals* that your system has been activated. And in that moment, you have a window.

Here's how to begin reclaiming that space:

1. **Feel It Before You Fix It**

    When you feel a charge rising, please don't rush to suppress or explain it. Notice:

    - Is my breath shallow or held?
    - Has my tone changed?
    - Is there heat, tension, urgency, or withdrawal?

    You're training your system to become aware of a shift *before* reacting.

2. **Name the State**

    You don't need to know the whole story, name the part:

    "This feels like a fight. I'm bracing."

    - *"My Inner Child voice is panicking."*
    - *"My Inner Parent voice is trying to take over."*

    Naming the state reduces the power of the trigger. You shift from *being inside it* to *witnessing it*.

3. **Regulate Before You Respond**

    Pause. Use one tool, just one:

    - Slow exhale (4–6 counts)
    - Press your feet into the floor
    - Soothing touch: hand on heart, or arms
    - Hum or gently sway

    This signals to your nervous system: *we're safe now.* From here, the Adult Self and Higher Self become accessible again.

4. **Ask the Deciding Question**

   Before speaking, ask: *"Who's about to speak? My past or my present?"*

   Then choose: do I want to speak from fear, from defence, or my true Self?

Trigger Awareness Log:

Each time you notice a strong reaction, jot it down:
- **Trigger moment:** What happened?
- **My reaction:** What did I feel, do, or say?
- **What voice took over?** (Inner Child / Inner Parent / Adult Self)
- **What belief may have been activated?**
- **How would I like to respond next time** — from my Higher Self?

Doing this just 2–3 times a week builds incredible awareness. Over time, you'll find that you're no longer reacting the same way. You're choosing, and your voice begins to reflect your *authentic self*, not just your old wounds.

WHEN AVOIDING PAIN CREATES MORE OF IT

Ironically, your Inner Parent often justifies your protective behaviours, telling you they are wise, necessary, or mature responses to life. But over time, you start to realise: these habits may protect you from immediate discomfort, but they also block your growth and deny you the very healing you genuinely need.

These unconscious patterns, rooted in past pain, create self-fulfilling cycles. What you fear, you end up repeating, not out of choice, but out of survival.

Here's how:

1. **You fear rejection, so you become overly agreeable.**
   - You say *"Yes"* when you mean *"No"*. You adapt, appease, and avoid waves.
   - But people never get to know the real you.

   Result: You feel unseen, misunderstood, and ultimately rejected. Not for who you are, but for the version you present.

2. **You fear conflict, so you suppress your needs.**
   - You avoid hard conversations. You internalise instead of expressing.
   - But resentment simmers beneath the surface.

   Result: Eventually, you explode or shut down, creating precisely the kind of conflict you were trying to avoid.

3. **You fear not being good enough, so you overachieve.**
   - You push harder, strive for perfection, never rest.
   - But the finish line keeps moving.

   Result: You burn out, feel like a failure, and the belief that *"I'm not enough"* gets reinforced.

4. **You fear being too much, so you silence or shrink your voice.**
   - You water yourself down, censor your truth.
   - But others don't hear your real needs or perspectives.

   Result: You feel invisible, which confirms your fear that you are "too much" to be accepted as you are.

5. **You fear abandonment, so you over-function in relationships.**
   - You become the helper, the fixer, the emotional caretaker.
   - But others experience this as controlling or needy.

   Result: They distance themselves, and you feel abandoned, again.

6. **You fear judgment, so you stay small or silent.**

    - You avoid being seen fully. You hide your true thoughts, talents, or emotions.
    - But this disconnects you from meaningful relationships.

    Result: You feel alone and believe no one truly understands you.

7. **You fear being powerless, so you try to control everything.**

    - You micromanage, fix, and anticipate every possible threat.
    - But people feel smothered or distrusted.

    Result: They push back, and you feel even more powerless.

8. **You fear emotional pain, so you numb yourself with distraction.**

    - You scroll, overwork, drink, eat, binge, and avoid stillness.
    - But the pain doesn't leave, it just waits.

    Result: You feel disconnected from yourself and life, and the pain eventually returns, louder.

9. **You fear being exposed, so you over-explain everything.**

    - You speak in circles, trying to justify or prove your worth.
    - But others tune out or lose interest.

    Result: You feel unseen and unheard, confirming your fear of being misunderstood.

10. **You fear being alone, so you stay in relationships that cause you harm.**

    - You tolerate mistreatment or emotional absence to avoid being alone.
    - But the relationship drains you, and your needs remain unmet.

    Result: You feel even lonelier than if you were truly alone.

These patterns aren't conscious choices, they're emotional reflexes, shaped by your past and embedded in your nervous system. You act from instinct, not intention.

But once you become aware of these loops, and learn how to update the beliefs beneath them, you regain the power to choose. You no longer have to live trapped by old fears. You can begin to speak, act, and lead from alignment, not avoidance.

WHY TALK THERAPY ALONE ISN'T ENOUGH

One of the most significant challenges in traditional talk therapy is that it primarily engages the conscious and preconscious layers of your mind, the parts of you that are already somewhat aware. You can explore your thoughts, describe your feelings, reflect on memories, and gain meaningful insight into your patterns. This can provide relief, clarity, and understanding.

However, the real roots of your behaviour, emotional pain, and reactivity often live beyond conscious awareness. The patterns that drive you don't originate in thought, they were formed in the subconscious and unconscious layers of the mind, where your protective responses, conditioned beliefs, and survival adaptations were shaped.

This is why talking alone often isn't enough to create lasting change. Insight can help you understand a pattern, yet still find yourself reacting the same way. To truly shift these deeper programs, you need to go beyond analysis and engage the body, the nervous system, and the brain's core wiring, because that is where the pattern is stored.

This is where neuroscience and neuroplasticity become essential. Neuroplasticity, the brain's ability to reorganise and form new neural pathways is the mechanism that allows you to change emotional reflexes, learned behaviours, and long-standing coping responses. Even protective adaptations formed in childhood can be rewired.

With the right tools, ones that work directly with the nervous system and neural pathways, you can interrupt automatic reactions and replace them with new responses. You can move from panic to steadiness, from people-pleasing to truth, from shutdown to presence.

Unlike talk therapy alone, which may take years to create shifts when trauma is involved, neuroscience-based methods reach the source of the pattern. Your brain is always active and available for transformation. No part lies dormant. When you intentionally activate neuroplasticity through subconscious repatterning, emotional release, and nervous system retraining, you stop merely talking about change and start experiencing it from the inside out.

WHY THE SUBCONSCIOUS ISN'T REACHED THROUGH LOGIC ALONE

One of the biggest misconceptions in personal growth is the belief that awareness is enough to create change. You can know a pattern, recognise it, analyse it, and still repeat it. That's because your reactions, impulses, and communication habits are shaped not by the conscious mind, but by the subconscious, where your emotional conditioning and protective strategies operate automatically.

The conscious mind is the part of you that reflects, reasons, and sets intentions. It says, *"I shouldn't take things personally," "I want to stay calm,"* or *"I won't abandon myself this time."* But the subconscious has its own language and its own logic. It doesn't respond to willpower or rational explanation.

This is why traditional talk therapy can hit a wall. You may intellectually understand your pattern, but still feel hijacked in the moment. You know better, but you still react. That's because the subconscious survival response is faster than your thoughts. It acts in a split second to protect you, often based on old, unresolved emotional experiences from the past. Until those subconscious memories are accessed through safety, nervous system regulation, and emotional integration, they remain active in the background, silently influencing your communication, tone, and self-perception.

The subconscious speaks through sensation, emotion, tension, withdrawal, people-pleasing, shutting down, defensiveness, appeasing, overachieving, rescuing, or reacting before you can think. The subconscious acts first, and the conscious mind explains it afterward. This is why you can know better and still repeat the same responses.

This is why neuroscience-based approaches, which work with the emotional brain, the nervous system, and subconscious reprogramming are so powerful. They reach the part of you that talking alone cannot access: the part that needs to feel safe, to release, and to update the old imprint that is still shaping your behaviour. When you communicate with the subconscious in its native language, the patterns that once felt automatic begin to soften, reorganise, and change.

Here's the key distinction:

Conscious Mind	Subconscious Mind
Logical, rational	Emotional, protective
Uses language and insight	Uses reflex and pattern
Voluntary memory (you can recall it)	Involuntary memory (automatic triggers)
Can reflect, observe and decide	Reacts instinctively, often before thought
Accessed through thinking and talking	Accessed through body, emotion, and safety

MINDSET DOESN'T REWIRE - EXPERIENCE DOES

Neuroplasticity, your brain's ability to rewire itself, is not driven by thought alone. It is shaped through **repeated, regulated emotional experience**. This means:

- You must experience **safety in the body**, not just say *"I'm safe."*
- You must activate your Adult Self to **observe and decide**
- You may **hear the guidance your Higher Self provides**, and act on it, while staying emotionally present
- You must be able to **name and observe a trigger** while remaining **in a regulated state**, so the brain learns a new outcome.

That's the recipe for change:

Safety + Awareness + New Experience = New Neural Wiring.

Your brain doesn't rewire through logic, it rewires when the emotional body says:

> *"This time, I wasn't abandoned."*
> *"This time, I could speak my truth and stay safe."*
> *"This time, I didn't run or collapse. I stayed."*

That's what creates new neural pathways.

And that's why mindset alone, no matter how powerful, isn't enough.

You need to feel the new experience in your nervous system.

You need your **Higher Self and Adult Self** present in the moment where your system used to collapse or defend.

FROM TRIGGERED TO TRUE: WHY THIS WORK CHANGES EVERYTHING

When you clear these subconscious patterns, when your nervous system is no longer hijacked by old fear, and inherited beliefs no longer rule your mind, your voice changes.

You speak more clearly because you're no longer filtering through fear.

You lead more confidently because you trust your instincts again.

You show up with presence because you're not bracing or performing.

This is the real outcome of deep emotional and subconscious work: not just peace within, but power in how you show up in the world.

Now that we've explored why mindset work and talk therapy alone can't fully resolve triggers and trauma, let's look at what *does* work, and why the integration of science, soul, and somatic healing creates lasting change.

WHY SCIENCE AND SOUL CREATE LASTING CHANGE

When it comes to fundamental transformation, the fastest path is not one or the other—it's both. Science and soul are not separate forces. They are complementary layers of the same human system. Your biology and your truth working in unison.

Science gives us the tools to rewire the brain. Through neuroplasticity, somatic regulation, and subconscious clearing, we can dissolve the automatic patterns that once ran our lives. However, the soul provides us with the compass—the Higher Self's voice that brings meaning, wisdom, and deeper alignment with who we truly are.

Neuroscience-based change is fast because it works directly with the systems that hold the problem: the subconscious mind, the nervous system, and the emotional body. But it's the soul, your Higher Self, that offers new beliefs to take their place. It is what makes the change sustainable, rooted not in performance or perfectionism, but in authenticity.

When you combine the precision of science with the guidance of your soul, healing is not just possible, it's permanent. This is the path to becoming not just regulated but aligned. Not just free from your past, but connected to your purpose.

~

In the next chapter, we'll explore exactly when the voice of your Higher Self becomes your guide, how this works, and how to make these rewiring experiences happen more consistently and quickly using neuroscience-based change.

By meeting your Inner Parent with compassion and boundaries, you begin transforming shame into safety. Reparenting doesn't erase the voice, it rewrites its role. Now let's integrate what this means for your self-talk and tone.

REFLECTION & INTEGRATION

Reflection Practice: Noticing My Internal Battle

Take a moment to reflect on a time recently when you felt emotionally overwhelmed or reactive.

Ask yourself:

- Which part of me was leading? My Inner Child, Inner Parent, or Adult Self?
- What did I most need in that moment? Soothing, safety, boundaries, rest, compassion?
- What belief might have been driving my reaction?

Integration Practice: Voice Mapping My Patterns

Choose one common emotional pattern you notice in yourself (e.g. people-pleasing, shutting down, defensiveness).

- When does it usually appear?

- Which voice drives it? Inner Child, Inner Parent, Adult Self or Higher Self?
- What does it sound like in your tone, language, or presence?
- What might your Higher Self want you to remember when this pattern arises again?

Awareness Prompt

"I know better, but I still react..."

Gently explore a moment where this felt true for you. What does that part of you still believe it must do to stay safe? What might it need instead?

Realignment Intention

This week, I will notice when I'm reacting from past programming and pause to ask:

"Is this belief still true for who I am now?"
"Can I invite my Higher Self or Adult Self to lead instead?"

10

WHAT REWIRES THESE PATTERNS – SCIENCE + SOUL

Now that you understand what's been running your responses, and why emotional triggers hijack your voice, the next question becomes:

How do you actually clear these patterns and return to your true voice?

The answer lies in integration. Not just insight. Not just effort. But a full-system recalibration of mind, body, emotion, and soul.

This is where science meets soul: where the grounded truth of neuroscience combines with the inner guidance of the Higher Self. When these forces align, transformation becomes not just possible, but permanent.

Below are the four core elements that work together to rewire old patterns and restore congruence, confidence, and clarity in how you speak, act, and lead:

1. **Neuroscience-Based Rewiring: Changing the Map of the Mind**

Your brain is not a fixed machine. It is an adaptable, learning organism. Every belief you hold is encoded in your brain as a neural pathway, a learned connection shaped by past experience, emotional intensity, and repetition. This is the domain of neuroplasticity, your brain's ability to adapt, reshape, and rewire itself throughout life. That voice in your head that says, *"I'm not safe to speak,"* or *"I have to earn love,"* isn't random. It's the imprint of repeated emotional experience.

When you engage in neuroscience-based rewiring such as my *PsycheIQ™ Alignment Method*, **emotional memory reconsolidation**, or **subconscious clearing techniques**, you're working directly with the subconscious, where the original pattern was formed; you go straight to the root. These processes reach the **subconscious**, where the original pattern was formed. Unlike years of talking through a problem or repeating affirmations that rarely take hold, these processes work at the root of the survival reflex.

Instead of layering affirmations on top of fear, you:

- Clear emotional imprints
- Update outdated programming
- Rewire core beliefs where they live: in your nervous system and subconscious.

You're not just thinking differently. You're feeling and responding differently because your neural map has changed at the root. This is why this work is faster and more lasting than years of talk therapy or mindset coaching. You don't just manage your reactions, you transform them.

2. **Emotional Resolution: Releasing the Charge Behind the Belief**

Most beliefs are not thoughts, they are **emotional memories**.

A sentence like *"I'm not enough"* is powered not by logic, but by past experiences of shame, rejection, or loss. It's anchored in pain:

- The moment you were ignored
- The time you were punished for expressing a need

- The heartbreak you never got to process.

You don't simply *think* it, you *feel* it:

- In your gut, your chest, your voice, your breath
- In your reflexes, defensiveness, or numbness
- In your hesitation to speak or trust yourself.

This is why, when you speak, you may:

- Feel your throat close
- Hear your voice tremble
- Pull back mid-sentence, apologising for having a need.

These aren't performance issues, they're emotional reflexes. And until the charge is cleared, they'll continue.

If you try to install a new belief without clearing the emotional charge beneath it, the nervous system will resist, because the old story still feels *true*.

Actual change happens when the original emotion is given space to complete, not intellectually, but somatically. This is **emotional resolution** and may happen through:

- Inner Child dialogue
- Somatic unwinding or breathwork
- Guided subconscious clearing
- A practitioner helping you reprocess the frozen emotion

When the charge dissolves, the story no longer controls you.

The belief no longer sticks.

The nervous system no longer flinches.

The voice returns to calm, grounded truth.

3. **Nervous System Regulation: Creating the Conditions for Change**

You cannot change your thoughts, voice, or beliefs if your **body is still braced for danger** and still feels under threat.

When you're in a **sympathetic (fight/flight)** or **dorsal (freeze/collapse)** state, your system is in protection mode. The prefrontal cortex (your conscious Adult Self) goes offline. The Higher Self becomes inaudible.

This is why nervous system regulation is not a "nice to have", it's *non-negotiable for transformation.*

When the body is regulated:

- The **prefrontal cortex** comes back online
- The **Adult Self** becomes available
- The **Higher Self** can guide your response
- New beliefs become possible and believable.

Simple tools, such as breath, grounding, vagus nerve activation, or sensory anchoring, send signals of **safety** to the body, promoting a sense of calm and well-being. And safety is what opens the door to **rewiring**.

Because only a calm system will accept a new truth.

4. **Higher Self Guidance: Seeding New Beliefs That Align with Truth**

Once the old story has been cleared, and your system is calm, a new belief can take root.

This is the role of the **Higher Self.**

Unlike the Inner Parent or Inner Child, the Higher Self doesn't operate through guilt, fear, shame, or pressure. It offers **gentle direction**, emotional congruence, and grounded truth. It says:

- *"You are safe to speak."*
- *"Your needs matter."*
- *"You are already whole."*

- "It's okay to be seen."

These aren't mantras you force yourself to believe, they are **restorative truths** you begin to *feel* as real.

And because the emotional charge has been cleared, and the body feels safe, these truths can **land**. They can be **accepted** by the subconscious and integrated into your identity.

This is how beliefs are not just replaced, they are **rewritten at the core**.

THIS ISN'T JUST BELIEF CHANGE - IT'S IDENTITY RESTORATION

And this is the path you are on.

Not just learning how to speak better…

But learning how to live from truth, not from trauma.

You are not simply learning how to think differently.

You are restoring the self that existed before fear distorted your truth.

You are reclaiming the voice that was silenced by trauma, shame, or survival.

You are not just rewiring. You are remembering who you are.

You are choosing to live in alignment with your whole self; emotionally, spiritually, neurologically.

This is not a surface shift.

It's a complete system return to:
- **Clarity** (you can now see the pattern)
- **Compassion** (you can now meet the pain without fusing with it)
- **Congruence** (your voice, body, and truth are aligned)

True transformation happens at the intersection of:

- **Science** (brain rewiring + nervous system flexibility)
- **Emotion** (resolution of the charge)
- **Presence** (regulation of the moment)
- **Soul** (guidance from your Higher Self).

This is what makes the change sustainable, because it happens at every level. Not just insight. Not just behaviour. But whole-system alignment.

THIS IS THE WORK WE DO INSIDE THE REWRITE & IGNITE™ PROGRAM

Everything you've explored so far, from emotional reactivity to voice distortion to rewiring through science and soul, is just the beginning.

Inside our **Rewrite & Ignite™** Program, we don't just talk about these patterns, we *clear* them.

Through neuroscience-based rewiring, emotional processing, and guided subconscious change, we help you:

- **Release** what's been driving your survival responses
- **Rebuild** emotional safety in your body
- **Realign** your identity with your truth.

This isn't about years of analysing. It's about weeks of *clearing*.

So, if you're ready to remove the blocks for good, and step into a new chapter of clarity, confidence, connection, and soul-led leadership, I invite you to explore the next level.

Visit ⇨ **RewriteAndIgnite.com** to learn more.

REFLECTION & INTEGRATION

Reflection Prompt: Where Am I Still Living from the Past?

Take a few moments to reflect on this question:

- In what area of my life do I still speak, act, or choose from an old pattern, not from who I am now?
- What belief, emotion, or reflex is still shaping my tone or presence in those moments?

Integration Inquiry: Feeling vs. Forcing the Change

Notice the difference between times when you've tried to think your way out of a pattern vs. when you've felt the shift in your body. Ask:

- What emotional charge still feels active in me?
- What part of me (Inner Child, Inner Parent) still needs to be heard, held, or updated?

Realignment Intention

This week, when I notice a reactive response rise in me, I will pause and ask:

- Has this pattern been cleared at the root or am I trying to manage it with effort alone?
- Can I invite my Higher Self to guide me through this, gently?

Higher Self Whisper

Close your eyes and breathe into your heart. Imagine your Higher Self placing a hand on your shoulder and saying:

- *"You are safe now. You don't need to protect yourself the same way anymore. I've got you."*

11

BUILDING EMOTIONAL SAFETY WITHIN

Emotional safety is not just about being calm or avoiding conflict. It's the internal sense that you are safe enough to **stay present** with your emotions, express your truth, and remain grounded even in moments of uncertainty. Without emotional safety, your nervous system stays on alert, your reactive parts take over, and your authentic voice is suppressed. Emotional safety is the **foundation** for authentic communication, personal growth, and leadership presence. You cannot grow where you do not feel safe. And you cannot speak your truth when your body believes it's still in danger.

EXTERNAL VS INTERNAL SAFETY

Many people wait for safety to come from the outside: from validation, approval, the "right" partner, or a conflict-free environment. I often refer to this as externalising your needs. However, genuine emotional safety is an internal process, one that involves internalising and meeting your own needs. This is not to say you can't be reliant on others, but it means you **rely on yourself first** by meeting your own needs.

It begins when your Adult Self becomes the **inner container** that holds space for the Inner Child's fears and the Inner Parent's criticisms, when your Adult Self is the observer and decision maker on what is best for your true self.

When your safety depends on others, you remain in emotional captivity. But when you learn to regulate, reassure, and stay with yourself through discomfort, you become your own safe home.

THE VOICES THAT UNDERMINE SAFETY

Your internal voices most often compromise emotional safety:

- The Inner Parent undermines safety by using fear, guilt, or control to get **compliance**
- The Inner Child feels unsafe when left **unsupported or unseen**
- The Inner Parent attacks, shames, or **sets unrealistic standards**.

When these voices dominate, your nervous system reads it as danger. Even if your outer world is calm, your inner world feels unstable. Recognising which voice is active gives you the power to shift back into the Adult Self, the only voice that can restore inner safety.

PRACTICES THAT BUILD INNER SAFETY (FOUNDATIONAL HABITS)

Safety is not a one-time achievement; it's a habit that requires ongoing attention and commitment. You build it through repeated, small actions that send your system the message: *"I am here. I am safe."*

- **Grounding** through the feet, breath, and body awareness
- Daily emotional **check-ins:** *"What am I feeling? What do I need?"*

- **Self-soothing rituals:** touch, warmth, gentle movement
- **Recognising false alarms:** *"This feels old. Am I reacting to the now, or the past?"* Over time, these practices rewire your nervous system to expect safety rather than threat.

ADULT SELF-REASSURANCE AS A NERVOUS SYSTEM REGULATOR

The Adult Self voice is the one that calms the system, not with denial or bypassing, but with **compassionate witnessing**. When fear arises, your Adult Self can say: *"I see you. That was scary. But we're okay now."* This is not a performance. It's a nervous system intervention. The tone of your internal voice matters. Reassurance from the Adult Self restores safety not just in thought, but in the body.

REPARENTING AS A SAFETY PRACTICE

Reparenting is not about fixing the Inner Child. It's about showing up consistently with curiosity, compassion, and presence. You begin to validate emotions instead of silencing them, meet needs instead of bypassing them, and create emotional continuity. You also learn to set boundaries with your Inner Parent, the harsh internal critic, by saying, *"That's not helpful right now."* Over time, this builds trust between your internal parts, and **trust is the root of safety.**

REBUILDING TRUST WITH YOURSELF

Emotional safety deepens as you prove to yourself that you won't abandon your truth. This happens when:

- You honour your *"No"* and speak it clearly
- You keep small promises to yourself
- You stop performing and start revealing

- You forgive quickly when you self-abandon and recorrect your course.

Trust is built not by perfection, but by presence. When you show up for yourself repeatedly, your system relaxes. **Your voice strengthens.**

WHY EMOTIONAL SAFETY IS THE FOUNDATION OF AUTHENTIC VOICE

When your system feels safe, your voice becomes congruent with your truth. You no longer speak from fear or perform to please. You speak from alignment. Emotional safety allows your Higher Self to come online and guide your communication. It will enable your Adult Self to choose words with care, express needs clearly, and navigate conflict with grounded presence. Without emotional safety, even your best intentions will be distorted by tone, defensiveness, or self-suppression. But with it, your voice becomes not just audible, but trustworthy.

~

Now that you've learned how emotional safety anchors your nervous system and voice, the next step is reclaiming the practices that build internal trust. The following prompts will help you create your own safe space.

REFLECTION & INTEGRATION

Reflection Prompt: Where Do I Still Outsource My Safety?

Take a few minutes to ask yourself gently:

- In what moments do I still wait for others to validate, soothe, or approve of me before I feel safe to speak, act, or rest?
- What part of me (Inner Child or Inner Parent) is trying to control or avoid those moments?

Integration Prompt: Rebuilding Trust with Myself

Ask yourself:

- What is one small way I could show myself today that I won't abandon my truth?
- What promise could I keep to myself that would rebuild trust, even a little?

Realignment Intention

This week, I will practise being my own safe home.

- I will listen to what I need
- I will speak to myself with a kind, regulating tone
- I will remind my nervous system: "You are safe. I'm here with you."

Higher Self Whisper

Imagine your Higher Self kneeling beside you and saying gently:

- *"You don't have to earn rest. You don't have to perform to be safe. You are allowed to be. I'm not going anywhere."*

Part IV

Speak It Like You Mean It

The return of your authentic, soul-aligned voice.

Now that you've cleared the noise, it's time to hear what your truth sounds like. In this part, you'll meet the voice of your Higher Self, the one that speaks with clarity, compassion, and courage. You'll learn how to express boundaries without guilt, communicate without collapse, and honour what you know. This is your voice, powerful, precise, and no longer afraid.

12

THE LANGUAGE OF THE HIGHER SELF

Do you recall the emotional tables from Chapter 4 *Natural Emotions* versus *Distorted Emotions*? When you begin to consistently hear and follow the guidance of your Higher Self, you'll notice yourself operating more and more from that *Natural Emotions* column. That's not a coincidence, it's because *Distorted Emotions* are the product of a dysregulated nervous system, while Natural Emotions arise when the system is calm, grounded, and connected. And it is only from this regulated space that the voice of the **Higher Self becomes available.**

You may experience the Higher Self in different ways. Some refer to it as their *gut instinct*, their *spirit*, *inner self* or their *intuitive self.* But no matter what you call it, the Higher Self is always present, a steady frequency signal that **never disappears**. The key is tuning in.

The voice of the Higher Self has a distinct signature:

- It is calm
- It is knowing
- It carries clarity without urgency
- It offers truth without fear
- It directs firmly, but never controls
- It feels emotionally attuned, grounded, and precise, yet gentle.

It doesn't shout. It rarely speaks in complete sentences. It whispers. It offers. It nudges. It delivers wisdom in a tone that feels like your own voice. Or sometimes, just slightly different from it. It arrives like a quiet inner *rightness*, often accompanied by a physical sensation of peace or alignment. There is **no panic, no rush, no pressure**. Just a knowing that moves you forward in service of your highest good.

You are **never disconnected** from this voice. Even in your darkest moments, the Higher Self does not abandon you. But it can feel that way, especially in times of intense inner conflict. Why? Because the part of you that *hears* the Higher Self—your Adult Self must be online. And when your system is overwhelmed by the power struggle between your Inner Parent and Inner Child, the **Adult Self often goes missing**. And when that happens, the channel becomes blocked.

The Higher Self speaks *through* the Adult Self, the part of your mind that is capable of pausing, witnessing, and making choices. So, if your Adult Self is offline, hijacked by emotional reactivity or drowned out by internal noise, the **guidance cannot come through**.

Ironically, the Higher Self often speaks *most clearly* when you're not even seeking it. You may be washing dishes, driving, walking, or just sitting quietly, and the message arrives, soft but certain. But when you're actively grasping for answers, mentally spiralling, emotionally charged, the signal seems silent. It's not that the guidance isn't there. It's that your mind is too loud to hear it.

To hear your Higher Self, the mind must be quiet. **Not empty**, just still enough to *receive*. That's why guidance rarely comes when you're frantically thinking, analysing, worrying, or rehashing old pain. The mind must stop *processing* so the soul can start *whispering*.

So, how do you hear the voice of the Higher Self when you're in the middle of chaos, when your Inner Child is panicking, your Inner Parent is lecturing, and your nervous system is firing on all cylinders?

You begin by **slowing down the system**. You calm the Inner Child. You soften the Inner Parent. You invite the Adult Self back into the room. You observe the agendas of each. And over time, you clear the old emotional noise that has been clogging your internal frequency.

You do this through meditation. Through breath. Through stillness. Through subconscious clearing. Through healing the emotional burdens you've been carrying like a backpack full of bricks. And slowly, gently, a new kind of voice emerges. Quieter. Wiser. Clearer.

It was never gone.

You just needed to make space to hear it.

HOW TO RECOGNISE THE HIGHER SELF IN REAL TIME

The Higher Self is like a radio signal. The frequency is always there, but you have to tune in. If the channel is filled with static (such as worry, fear, or stress), the message won't come through clearly. But when you still the noise, even for a moment, you can catch the message. And it always comes in the moment you need it most.

The Higher Self doesn't usually announce itself with a grand trumpet. It arrives subtly through presence, not performance. So, how do you know when it's speaking?

Physical cues:
- Your breath becomes **slower and fuller**

- Your body feels **grounded**. Less tension, more stability
- Your heart rate **slows**; you *feel in* your body, not racing above it.

Emotional cues:

- There's **no urgency**. No grasping. Just calm knowing
- **Compassion** is present, not only toward others, but toward yourself
- There is a **softness** around the message, even when the truth is sharp.

Language cues:

- It uses **direct, clear language** without judgment or control
- It doesn't speak in **absolutes or extremes**
- It doesn't **argue,** it offers
- Its tone is **assured**, but never **forceful**.

HOW THE HIGHER SELF SPEAKS IN EVERYDAY LIFE

In moments of danger or survival:

- *"Take the next exit now."* (Later, you find out there was an accident on your planned route)
- *"Don't go in there."* (Your body tenses before your mind registers why)
- *"Turn around. Go home."* (No explanation, but your whole system knows it's right).

In deep grief or emotional collapse:

- *"Just get up. Move your body."* (The voice feels steady, calm, not forceful, just insistent)
- *"Breathe. One thing at a time."* (You follow it without thinking, and it calms you)

- *"You are not alone."* (The voice you hear when everything else feels numb).

In moments of temptation or sabotage:

- *"You've been here before. You know how this ends."* (Said not with shame, but awareness)
- *"This will numb the pain, but won't solve it."* (Gently interrupting the impulse).

In a relationship or communication:

- *"Say the hard thing, with love."* (When your Inner Child wants to avoid conflict)
- *"It's time to forgive, for you, not for them."* (A soft nudge toward emotional freedom)
- *"Pause. Listen. Don't rush to defend."* (The voice that helps you stay present in a challenge).

In leadership or decision-making:

- *"This isn't aligned anymore, let it go."* (Even if your mind resists, your body feels the truth)
- *"Reach out to them. Now."* (Later, they tell you they needed someone at that exact moment)
- *"It's not fear, it's growth calling."* (A calm voice reframing anxiety as expansion).

The key difference?

The Higher Self doesn't *beg, panic, or punish*. It speaks with **knowing**.

It gives *direction, not demands*.

And the moment you follow it, even slightly, the nervous system often begins to settle.

WHY THE HIGHER SELF ISN'T ALWAYS LOUD

In a world filled with noise, internal and external, the Higher Self often feels too quiet to compete. That's not because it's weak. It's because it doesn't shout to be heard. It doesn't need to.

- The Higher Self **whispers**, not out of fear, but out of confidence. It knows its truth, so it doesn't need to yell
- It doesn't judge; it **guides**
- It helps you **evolve and grow**
- It never forces. It only **invites**
- It doesn't rush. It waits for **stillness**.

This is why it's often missed when you are:

- In sympathetic arousal (fight/flight)
- Caught in looping thoughts or generally processing information
- Reactive, defensive, or emotionally overwhelmed.

PRACTISING LISTENING TO HIGHER SELF SPEECH

To listen to your Higher Self, you must first *recognise* when you're not. Most of us speak from fear, habit, or a sense of survival, especially under stress.

Here's how it can sound different on the next page:

Survival Voice	Higher Self Voice
"You messed that up."	"That didn't go how you hoped. What can you learn?"
"They're going to reject you."	"Not everyone is for you, and that's okay. Your truth still matters."
"You have to fix this, or you'll be punished."	"You can face this. You're not alone."

Practice reframing in real scenarios to listen:

Conflict:

    Survival: *"I can't believe they said that to me."*

    Higher Self: *"That hurt and I can choose how I respond."*

Leadership:

    Survival: *"I have to get this perfect."*

    Higher Self: *"I will do my best and lead with clarity, not fear."*

Boundaries:

    Survival: *"I don't want them to be mad."*

    Higher Self: *"This matters to me and I can express it respectfully."*

HOW TO STRENGTHEN THE CONNECTION

The more you choose presence over panic, the more clearly you'll hear your Higher Self's voice.

Here are simple ways to build the bridge:

Daily nervous system regulation

- Breathwork (slow, rhythmic breathing)
- Grounding (bare feet on earth, hand on heart)
- Gentle movement (yoga, somatics, walking).

Higher Self check-ins

- Ask: *"What would truth say right now?"*
- Journal: *"What part of me is speaking? Inner Child, Inner Parent, Adult Self or Higher Self?"*
- Practice small choices from Higher Self (how you respond to emails, boundaries, self-care).

Language shift rituals

- Use a calming tone in self-talk
- Pause before reacting in conversations
- Speak from grounded truth, not urgency.

WHY THIS MATTERS IN COMMUNICATION, LEADERSHIP & LIFE

When your Higher Self leads your voice, everything changes.

You become someone who communicates not just with confidence, but with **congruence**. Your words match your values. Your actions match your words. Your tone matches your presence. You speak from wholeness, not from wounding.

In **communication**, you speak with compassion and clarity, even in difficult moments.

In leadership, you hold presence, boundaries, and vision without needing to dominate or perform.

In life, you feel anchored, guided not by reaction, but by truth.

This is the voice that earns **trust**.

This is the tone that inspires **growth**.

This is the language of **who you truly are**.

REFLECTION & INTEGRATION

Tuning into the Language of Your Higher Self

Daily Awareness Prompt:

At the end of each day, take a moment to reflect:

- When did I feel most connected to calm, clear inner guidance today?
- What did that voice sound or feel like in my body?
- Did I follow it? Or override it with fear, urgency, or doubt?

Journal Prompt – Meeting the Higher Self in Real Time:

Think back to a moment recently when you felt anxious, uncertain, or emotionally reactive.

- What voice was leading in that moment? Inner Child, Inner Parent, Adult Self or Higher Self?
- What did each part want to say?
- If the Higher Self had been leading, what might it have said instead?

Practice – Rewriting the Survival Voice:

Choose one recurring internal statement you often hear when stressed or afraid.

Examples:

- *"I'm going to mess this up."*
- *"They're not going to accept me."*
- *"I have to fix this or else…"*

Now, rewrite this statement through the voice of your Higher Self.

Examples:

- *"Even if I don't get this perfect, I can handle the outcome with grace."*
- *"I am not for everyone and that's okay."*
- *"I can face this moment with clarity and trust myself."*

Repeat your Higher Self reframe out loud, gently, calmly, and with grounded presence.

Self-Awareness Check-In:

Pause throughout the day and ask:

- *"What part of me is speaking right now? My fear, my past, or my Higher Self?"*
- *"What would truth say in this moment?"*

Let that voice guide your next action or response.

Higher Self Connection Practice:

Each morning or evening, take 2–3 minutes to breathe deeply and ask inwardly:

- *"Higher Self, what do I need to hear today?"*
- Write down the first calm, clear message you sense or feel, without forcing.

This is how the relationship strengthens: not through perfection, but through presence.

Alignment Intention:

I will create more quiet moments in my day so that I can hear, feel, and follow the calm, guiding voice of my Higher Self.

13

CONSCIOUS BOUNDARIES AND SOUL INTEGRITY

Boundaries are not just logistical decisions, they are soul declarations. Every boundary you set is a line drawn not just in time, energy, or space… but in identity. It says, *"This is who I am. This is what I need to stay true to myself."*

To many, boundaries feel like walls. Something to keep others out. But in truth, **a conscious boundary is a doorway to deeper authenticity.** It's not about punishment or rejection. It's about alignment. It's a statement that says: *"I will no longer abandon myself to keep the peace."*

Boundaries are soul work because they force us to get clear on what we value, what we honour, and what we will no longer tolerate. They strip away the performance and the people-pleasing masks, asking instead:

- *"What does my truth need in this moment?"*
- *"What serves my expansion, not just my safety?"*

Without clear boundaries, we leak energy. We say *"Yes"* when our mind and body say, *"No"*. We over-explain, over-give, and override our truth to avoid discomfort, loss and disconnection with others. And with every act of self-abandonment, our authenticity dims, not because it's gone, but because we stopped protecting it.

But with soul-aligned boundaries, your essence begins to shine again. **You stop managing how others feel about you and start honouring how you feel within yourself.**

And the ripple effect is profound:

- Your relationships become more transparent and more respectful
- Your leadership gains integrity and strength
- Your inner voice becomes louder, calmer, and more stable, because it knows you will honour it
- Most of all, your self-love and self-worth grow the more you establish soul-led boundaries.

> *Every time you set a conscious boundary,*
> *you honour the truth of who you are.*

This is not about being harsh or cold. The **most powerful boundaries are set with clarity and compassion**, not with anger, but with certainty. Not to punish others, but to protect your peace. It is about checking in and hearing the guidance *"Is this ok or right for me?"*.

This is why setting boundaries is one of the most courageous acts of soul integrity. It asks you to risk disapproval in service of truth. It teaches your nervous system that safety doesn't come from pleasing. It comes from alignment.

And when you begin to live this way—boundaried, clear, heart-aligned, your communication changes. You speak less from fear, more from the centre. You stop asking for permission and start living with purpose.

THE NERVOUS SYSTEM AND BOUNDARIES

Many of the struggles we experience with boundaries aren't logical, they're physiological. **People-pleasing, over-explaining, over-functioning, or saying "Yes" when you mean "No" are not personality flaws.** They are survival reflexes that have been wired into your nervous system over time.

At some point in your early experience, especially in childhood, you learned that safety, approval, or **love depended on compliance**. You may have been praised for being easy to get along with, agreeable, helpful, or quiet. You may have witnessed or experienced conflict being punished, emotions being dismissed, or your own needs being shamed. And your system adapted. It decided: *"It's safer to please than to upset. It's safer to go along than to speak up."*

These adaptations are brilliant for survival. But over time, **what once kept you safe becomes the very pattern that keeps you stuck**. You stay silent when you need to speak. You agree when your body screams *"No."* You explain, justify, or soften your truth, not because you don't know what it is, but because your nervous system has equated truth with threat.

This is why **setting boundaries often feels unsafe, even when you know it's the right thing to do**. It's not that you're weak or unclear. It's that your body is still carrying the imprint of danger around self-expression.

The good news is: this imprint can change. And it doesn't require years of effort. It requires nervous system safety.

Nervous system regulation is the missing link in boundary work. Remember, when your system is regulated—grounded, present, and connected, your prefrontal cortex is online. Your Adult Self is present. And your Higher Self becomes accessible. From this place, you can speak clearly without collapsing. You can say *"No"* without guilt. You can tolerate someone's disappointment without abandoning your truth.

Regulation allows for a new experience of boundaries:

- You don't need to yell, because your calm presence holds weight
- You don't need to justify, because your *"No"* is enough
- You don't need to shrink or puff up, because you are rooted in your worth.

When the nervous system feels safe, your voice can speak from truth, not trauma.

This is why learning to regulate your system is essential to setting boundaries with integrity. It gives you access to the part of you that can pause, assess, and respond, rather than react from fear.

Boundaries are not about power over others. They are about power *within* yourself, the power to choose your truth over your programming.

THE VOICES BEHIND WEAK OR RIGID BOUNDARIES

Every time you set (or avoid setting) a boundary, you are not just responding to the moment, you are also responding from within. Your boundary behaviour is often shaped not by logic, but by the **dominant inner voice** running the conversation inside you.

When your Inner Child is leading, you might say *"Yes"* when you mean *"No,"* simply to avoid the fear of rejection, disapproval, or being left out. When your Inner Parent takes charge, boundaries can become rigid, overly moralising, or filled with resentment and control. If your Inner Parent dominates, you may set a boundary, only to immediately attack yourself for doing so.

By contrast, when your Higher Self is present, your boundaries are calm, clear, and aligned. They are not aggressive or apologetic, they reflect the truth.

Understanding which voice is currently active helps you shift from reactivity to conscious choice. You begin to recognise: *"Ah, that's my Inner Child afraid to upset someone,"* or *"That's the Inner Parent guilting me again."* With that awareness, your Adult Self can step in and course-correct, allowing your Higher Self to lead with integrity.

Inner Voice	Boundary Pattern
Inner Child	Avoids conflict, says yes to prevent rejection, prioritises keeping the peace at all costs. Feels unsafe to upset others or be misunderstood.
Inner Parent	Becomes rigid, judgmental, or controlling. Sets boundaries with moral superiority, resentment, or blame. Enforces instead of communicates. Allows the boundary, but punishes you after. Voices like: *"That was too much." "You're selfish." "Who do you think you are?"*
Higher Self	Sets boundaries with clarity, firmness, and compassion. No performance, no guilt, no need for lengthy justifications. Just aligned truth.

Boundaries aren't just about behaviour, they are a reflection of your **internal leadership**. And the more aware you become of who's speaking inside, the more power you have to return to the voice that honours your truth without apology: your Higher Self.

Here's a scripted example illustrating how different inner voices might respond in a boundary-setting moment, followed by how it sounds when the Higher Self leads.

Scenario: A colleague asks you to stay late again, even though it's affecting your wellbeing.

1. **Inner Child (Fearful, Avoidant)**

   "Um... okay, I guess I can stay again. I don't want to let you down."

   Inner story: "If I say no, they won't like me. I might get in trouble."

2. **Inner Parent (Rigid, Controlling)**

   "Seriously? This is the third time. You need to respect my time."

   Inner story: "People should know better. I have to protect myself by being firm, or I'll be taken advantage of."

3. **Inner Parent (Self-critical, Doubting)**

   (After setting the boundary)

   "Maybe I shouldn't have said that. What if they think I'm selfish?"

   Inner story: "You don't have the right to put yourself first. You should be more accommodating."

4. **Adult Self (Calm, Clear, Compassionate) with guidance from Higher Self**

   "I know this is important, but I won't be able to stay late today. I've been running on empty and need to honour my limits so I can show up fully tomorrow."

   Inner story: "I can honour my wellbeing and still be respectful. This is *not selfish, it's sustainable."*

Notice how the **tone**, the **energy**, and even the **word choice** shift dramatically depending on which voice is speaking. The **Adult Self** doesn't attack or collapse. It simply speaks truth, with care for all involved.

BOUNDARIES ARE NOT WALLS - THEY ARE BRIDGES

Most people misunderstand boundaries as something harsh or confrontational—a wall that pushes others away. But actual, soul-aligned boundaries are not barriers of separation. They are bridges that protect the connection. They honour your truth while allowing others to meet you in it, if they're willing.

Boundaries built from unhealed pain tend to be rigid, defensive, or reactive:

- *"I've had enough of you. Don't ever speak to me like that again."*
- *"You always cross the line. I'm done."*

These responses may feel temporarily empowering, but they often emerge from emotional charge, from the wounded Inner Child or the rigid Inner Parent trying to regain control. In these moments, the boundary may sound like an attack, a withdrawal, or an ultimatum, and the relationship suffers as a result.

By contrast, **soul-aligned boundaries** come from the Higher Self and the Adult Self. They are grounded, transparent, and emotionally honest, not performative, not punishing. They preserve your integrity **while leaving space for respectful connection**. They consider the needs and protection of the Inner Child and the Inner Parent, which starts to settle purely because it has a governing body taking care of it.

You are not setting boundaries against people. You are setting boundaries for your wholeness.

These kinds of boundaries don't destroy connection, they clarify it. They help you honour your needs without collapsing or controlling. They model self-respect, not self-defence.

Let's look at the difference:

Reactive Boundary (Wall)	Conscious Boundary (Bridge)
"You can't talk to me like that."	"When that tone comes up, I feel unsafe, I'd like us to slow down."
"Stop asking me to stay late."	"I need to leave on time today, I've got to honour my energy."
"Don't bring your drama here."	"I want to support you, but I can't hold space when I'm drained."

The tone of a boundary is as crucial as its content. When spoken from presence, not protection, a boundary becomes a moment of *alignment*, not a weapon of defence.

SOUL INTEGRITY: LIVING ALIGNED WITH WHAT YOU KNOW

At its core, **integrity is not about being perfect**, it's about being whole. It's not a moral standard to measure up to; it's a state of internal congruence. Soul integrity means that your *inner knowing* and your *outer expression* are aligned, that you are no longer betraying yourself to maintain peace, please others, or perform a version of who you think you should be.

You know this feeling already.

You've felt it when you said *"Yes"* when you meant *"No."*

When you stayed quiet to avoid conflict, but walked away resentful.

When you kept a relationship, job, or dynamic going, long after your inner wisdom whispered: *"This isn't right anymore."*

> *Integrity doesn't just live in your words,
> it lives in your nervous system.*

When you act in contradiction to your truth, your body knows. Your soul feels it. That internal dissonance doesn't just create anxiety or confusion, it quietly drains your energy, weakens your voice, and eats away at your sense of self.

By contrast, **when you act in alignment with your truth**, your system relaxes. Your energy stabilises. Your voice softens but strengthens. You no longer feel like you're performing your life. You are *living it.*

Signs You Are Living in Soul Integrity:

- You say *"No"* without guilt, because your *"Yes"* is now sacred
- You no longer over-explain your boundaries. Clarity replaces apology
- You end misaligned work or relationships, not with drama, but with grace
- You hold firm boundaries without resentment, because they are rooted in self-respect, not fear
- You feel calm after hard conversations, because you didn't abandon yourself to keep the peace.

Living in soul integrity isn't a one-time decision/ It's a daily return to yourself. It's choosing, again and again, not to abandon your truth for temporary approval. And when you do fall out of alignment (as we all do), it's having the courage to come home to yourself, without shame, without self-punishment, and begin again.

When your Higher Self leads, your boundaries become clear, and your life begins to align with your truth.

WHEN BOUNDARIES ARE RESISTED OR MISUNDERSTOOD

One of the most uncomfortable parts of boundary work is this:

Sometimes, when you begin to honour your truth, other people don't like it.

They may resist.

They may misunderstand.

They may call you selfish, dramatic, or "too much."

But this doesn't mean you're doing something wrong.

It often means you're doing something new.

And new creates disruption, especially when your old patterns benefited others at your expense.

If you've spent years saying *"Yes"* when you wanted to say *"No"*…

If you've kept the peace at the cost of your truth…

If you've been the fixer, the appeaser, the over-functioner…

Then your shift will create a ripple.

People who were once comforted by your compliance may now feel discomfort in your clarity.

Your voice may rattle people who relied on your silence.

And people who benefited from your overgiving may label your boundaries as abandonment.

But their reaction does not determine your alignment.

Growth Brings Resistance, and resistance is not proof that you were wrong. It is a sign that the system is adjusting.

When you shift a pattern, others are forced to confront their own, and not everyone is ready to meet that discomfort.

Boundaries test relationships, not to break them, but to reveal whether they can meet the real you.

The purpose of your Adult Self is not to preserve someone else's comfort, it's to honour your integrity.

What to Remember in These Moments:

- You can be clear and kind, without collapsing
- You can love people and still say *"No"*
- You can cause disappointment and still be in integrity
- You can be misunderstood and still be whole.

A boundary is not a rejection of others. It's a reclamation of yourself.

HIGHER SELF BOUNDARY SCRIPTS

Here are some reworded examples of what it sounds like to set boundaries from the Higher Self on the next page:

Situation	Old Script (Fear/Survival)	Adult & Higher Self Script
Someone oversteps your time	"I guess I can squeeze it in..."	"Thanks for asking, I'm not available today."
Emotional manipulation	"I didn't mean to upset you!"	"I care about how you feel, but I also need space when things get heated."
Work pressure	"I'll just get it done somehow."	"That deadline won't work for me, let's find an alternative."

WHAT IT SOUNDS LIKE WHEN YOUR BOUNDARIES ARE MET WITH RESISTANCE, MISUNDERSTANDING, GUILT OR EVEN ANGER

Here are several sample scripts and dialogue examples for when your boundary is met with resistance, misunderstanding, guilt, or even anger, so you can stay clear and compassionate, without collapsing into old patterns:

When someone reacts with guilt:

"Oh wow... I didn't realise you felt that way. I guess I'm just a terrible friend, then."

Adult Self Response: *"I hear that this is hard to hear. That doesn't mean you're a bad friend. It just means I'm being honest about what I need right now. I value this relationship, and I'm naming this so it can stay strong."*

When someone gets defensive:

"Well, I guess I can't say anything around you anymore!"

Adult Self Response: *"That's not what I'm asking for. I want an open conversation, but I also want to feel safe and respected. This is about finding a way to talk where we both feel heard."*

When someone pushes back or pressures:

"Come on, don't be like that. Just do it. It's not a big deal."

Adult Self Response: *"It may not feel big to you, but it's important to me. I'm learning to honour that, even when it's uncomfortable."*

When someone accuses you of being selfish:

"Wow. You've changed. You only think about yourself now."

Adult Self Response: *"I am changing, and part of that means I'm learning to take care of myself in ways I didn't before. That doesn't mean I don't care about you. It just means I'm trying to show up more honestly."*

When someone tries to guilt you:

"After everything I've done for you, this is how you treat me?"

Adult Self Response: *"I appreciate everything you've done, and I still need to make choices that are right for me now. This isn't about the past, it's about how I stay in integrity with myself."*

When someone withdraws or gives the silent treatment:

(No words, just distance or passive withdrawal)

Adult Self Response (internal reminder or gentle approach): *"Their reaction is not my responsibility to manage. I can be available for conversation when they're ready, but I don't need to chase or shrink to be loved."*

Optional message:

"I notice some distance. If you want to talk, I'm open. I care about this relationship, and I also need to stay true to myself."

Reminder Phrase for Your Inner Dialogue:

"I can be loving and have boundaries at the same time."
"Their reaction is information, not instruction."
"If I stay kind and clear, I'm still in integrity."

~

Setting boundaries from your Higher Self is not a rejection, it's a return to self-respect. When your nervous system feels safe, your *"No"* becomes an act of alignment. Now, we'll explore how to embody that clarity.

REFLECTION & INTEGRATION

Journal Reflection – Listening to My Boundary Voice

Take a quiet moment and reflect:

- When was the last time I said *"Yes"* when I really meant *"No"*?
- What part of me was speaking in that moment? My Inner Child, Inner Parent, Adult Self or Higher Self?
- What did I fear would happen if I honoured my truth?
- What would my Higher Self have said or done instead?

Integration Prompt – Rewriting My Boundary Script

Think of a boundary you've been afraid to set.

Write out how you've been avoiding it. What words you've used (or haven't used).

Now rewrite it from the voice of your Higher Self.

Maintain a calm, grounded, and clear tone.

Example:

> Old version: *"I don't know... I guess I can help again."*
>
> Higher Self version: *"I care about you, and I'm not available for that right now. I need to protect my energy."*

Awareness Practice – Noticing My Boundary Reflexes

Over the next 3 days, notice how you respond in situations where your needs, time, or truth are being tested.

Ask yourself in real time:

- Am I speaking from fear, habit, or alignment?
- What am I afraid will happen if I say no or speak honestly?
- What emotion is rising in my body when I think about setting a boundary? Guilt, fear, panic, shame?
- What does my nervous system need right now to feel safe enough to speak truthfully?

Higher Self Check-In – Before the Boundary Conversation

Before a challenging conversation or moment where you'll need to honour a boundary, pause and ask:

- *"What does truth sound like here?"*
- *"What does love sound like toward me and others?"*
- *"What does my Inner Child need to feel safe? And how can I protect that without collapsing?"*

Then breathe, slow down, and speak from that grounded place.

Realignment Reminder – After a Difficult Boundary

If someone reacts poorly to your boundary, take a moment to realign inwardly. Say to yourself:

- *"Their discomfort doesn't mean I was wrong."*
- *"My job is to stay in integrity, not to manage their emotional process."*
- *"I can be kind and still say no."*

Write down how you feel after standing in your truth. Let yourself notice the difference between guilt and growth.

Ongoing Intention - Anchoring Soul-Led Boundaries

Set this intention and revisit it daily for one week:

"I will speak from my centre, not from fear. I will let my boundaries reflect who I truly am, not who I've been trained to be."

Part V

The Integration Code

Living, leading, and loving from truth, not trauma.

Healing isn't the end of the journey. It's the beginning of alignment. In this final part, you'll integrate everything you've learned so far: how to lead with integrity, speak with congruence, and embody the presence of someone who no longer performs, but is. You'll build a daily practice of returning to your truth and discover what it means to live from soul, even when the old patterns whisper. This is the shift that sticks, because it's who you've always been.

14

RECLAIMING YOUR AUTHENTIC VOICE

Your voice is more than just the words you speak. It's the energy, clarity, truth, and presence behind them. Most people speak from a place of survival, performance, or programming, without realising it. To reclaim your authentic voice means to speak from your inner alignment, where your truth meets grounded presence.

> *Authentic voice is not just about what you say, it's about where you speak from.*

WHY YOUR VOICE WAS HIDDEN (AND WHY THAT'S NOT YOUR FAULT)

Many of us learned to silence our voices in order to stay safe or even survive. Through trauma, cultural norms, or familial dynamics, we adapted. We said what was acceptable. We swallowed our needs. We learned that expressing our truth could come with a cost.

This wasn't your fault; it was your nervous system trying to protect you. But now you are ready to speak from truth, not fear.

Your authentic voice feels clear, grounded, and aligned. The distorted voice feels either collapsed or overblown.

Your authentic voice respects the truth of your experience without shaming or sugarcoating. It invites connection without performance.

When your Higher Self is present, your voice becomes wise, compassionate, and steady. You are no longer reacting from pain or posturing for approval. You speak with intention, presence, and truth, even in challenge. This voice is not loud, but it is powerful.

Voice distortion appears in everyday speech, such as over-apologising, performing, avoiding, and defending. Examples: *"Sorry, I just thought..."* becomes *"Here's what I'd like to offer."*

The goal isn't perfect speech. It is presence. It is honesty. It's speaking from the part of you that doesn't need to prove or please.

In high-stakes or emotionally charged moments, your nervous system may be inclined to react first. Pause.

Ground yourself. Ask. *"What part of me is speaking?"* Return to the Adult Self. Let the Higher Self guide the tone and truth.

Speaking your truth is vulnerable because it exposes your inner world to others. But healing happens through visibility.

You reclaim your voice not just by speaking, but by being willing to be seen in your truth, even if it shakes.

Remember: What truth wants is to be spoken, even if it's scary!

YOUR VOICE AS LEADERSHIP

This Is the Voice That Was Always Yours

Leadership isn't about volume. It's about alignment. When you speak from authenticity, others feel safe, inspired, and invited into clarity.

Your voice becomes a tuning fork, not just for ideas, but for emotional resonance and shared purpose.

Reclaiming your authentic voice isn't about becoming someone new. It's about remembering who you were before fear taught you to shrink.

Your voice is the instrument of your soul. When you speak from truth, you don't just communicate, you resonate.

~

As you learn to lead with your authentic voice, your words stop performing and start resonating. This is the moment your inner congruence becomes visible in the world. Let's explore what that looks like in real life.

REFLECTION & INTEGRATION

Journal Reflection – When Did I Stop Speaking Freely?

Take a quiet moment to reflect:

- Can I recall a time when I silenced my voice to stay safe, be liked, or avoid conflict?
- What did I fear would happen if I had spoken my truth?
- What belief did I form in that moment about using my voice?
- Is that belief still running my communication today?

Daily Practice – Checking Who's Speaking

For the next three days, pause at least once during any key conversation and ask:

- What part of me is speaking? Inner Child, Inner Parent, Adult Self, or Higher Self?
- Am I speaking from performance, protection, or presence?
- How does my body feel as I speak? Tight, soft, braced, grounded?

Voice Reframe Prompt – From Distortion to Truth

Choose one phrase or tone you often use that feels distorted or inauthentic.

For example:

"Sorry, I just thought…"

Now rewrite it from your authentic voice:

"Here's something I'd like to share."

Repeat this reframe aloud. Let it land in your body. Practice it during your day.

Grounding Practice – Speak After the Breath

Before speaking in emotionally charged moments, practise this micro-pause:

- Inhale slowly. Exhale fully.
- Feel your feet on the floor.
- Ask yourself: *"What does my Higher Self want to say?"*

Let that voice, not your survival reflex, guide your next words.

Integration Prompt – **My Voice in Leadership**

Ask yourself:

- Where in my life am I still dimming or distorting my voice to be accepted or avoid discomfort?
- What would change in my relationships, leadership, or self-worth if I let my true voice lead, even softly?
- What fear comes up when I imagine being fully seen and heard?
- What does my Higher Self want me to know about that fear?

Intention Anchor – **Voice as Soul**

Set this intention today and repeat it often:

> *"My voice is sacred. I don't need to shout or shrink. I need to speak from my truth."*

Reminder Phrase – **When It Feels Scary to Be Heard**

- *"My voice is not a threat, it's a truth."*
- *"If I speak with presence, I am safe, even in discomfort."*
- *"What truth wants is to be spoken, even if my voice shakes."*

15

INTEGRATING THE ARCHITECTURE: LIVING THE SHIFT

When you learn to embrace all four voices; the Inner Child, Inner Parent, Adult Self, and Higher Self, you activate a congruent, spiritually centred human being that is resilient and can flow through the challenges of intense emotional roller coaster rides, threats to your survival, and you no longer live on default.

When you heal your old subconscious patterns and survival reflexes, you give way for the Adult Self to emerge and be guided by the Higher Self. Your triggers become scars rather than open wounds, your nervous system relaxes quickly to events, and you make conscious decisions going forward.

You no longer believe every voice in your mind, you listen, then lead.

With time, the Inner Child is cared for. The Inner Parent is regulated and evolving. The Adult Self is active and observant, and the Higher Self leads the inner growth in your life. This is proper integration, enlightenment, and living authentically in accordance with your highest purpose on earth.

THE COLLAPSE BEFORE RESURRECTION

There often comes a moment on the healing path when the Inner Parent, long seen as the authority within, **begins to break down.**

Not because you've failed.

But because the life it was trying to control no longer matches reality.

The Inner Parent's role, for many years, has been to protect you, often through rigid control, perfectionism, and idealised visions of success, safety, and survival. It creates a blueprint: a projected image of how life *should* unfold. *"If I do everything right, I'll be safe." "If I work hard enough, I'll be loved." "If I stay in control, I won't be hurt again."*

But at some point, that projected image shatters.

Life throws something unexpected, a loss, betrayal, illness, collapse, or truth you can no longer suppress, and the Inner Parent **loses its grip on the story it built.** Suddenly, the strategies that once kept you safe stop working. The illusion of control disintegrates.

And this is where the **collapse begins.**

The Inner Parent, once rigid and commanding, now enters a state of shock, grief, or paralysis. It can't fix what's happening. It can't prevent what's unfolding. Its vision of life has fractured. And in that moment, something profound is revealed:

You were never truly in control.

Not in the way your Inner Parent believed.

This moment is often terrifying. It can feel like death. The death of the life you thought you were building. But beneath the collapse lies an invitation:

To resurrect.

To allow the Higher Self, the wise, soul-led voice within you, to take its rightful place as the guide of your life.

The collapse of the Inner Parent is not a failure; it is a natural part of the process.

It is a sacred rupture.

It is the gateway to truth.

Because only when the rigid control breaks... can surrender begin.

Only when the mind lets go... can the soul rise up.

Only when the projected image dissolves... can you finally see reality through the eyes of your Higher Self.

This is the turning point.

From living by survival rules... to living by soul guidance.

From being driven by protection... to being led by purpose.

From managing life... to trusting life.

Let the Inner Parent grieve. Let it mourn its lost identity, its shattered ideals. **But do not let it take back the lead.**

Instead, offer it the support it never had. Invite the Adult Self to step in as the new inner authority. And allow the Higher Self to guide what comes next.

Because this is not the end, it is your **resurrection**.

The beginning of life, not ruled by fear, but aligned with your **truth**.

Your **voice**.

Your **soul**.

LIVING FROM SOUL INTEGRITY

*Soul integrity isn't about perfection.
It's about congruence.*

It's the deep alignment between what you believe, what you feel, what you know, and how you show up in the world.

Many people live in a state of inner fragmentation. Saying *"Yes"* when they mean *"No,"* pleasing others while silently resenting, holding back truth out of fear, or speaking truth with an edge of unhealed pain. These are not moral failures. They are survival patterns. But over time, they erode self-trust and dim the voice of the Higher Self.

Soul integrity begins when you make a new choice:

To live from alignment, not performance. From truth, not protection. From consciousness, not conditioning.

FROM HEALING TO LEADING

The inner work you've done throughout this book hasn't just been about resolving pain or understanding patterns, it's been about reclaiming the *leader within you*. Not necessarily in the corporate or public sense (though it may show up there), but in the truest sense: the ability to lead *yourself* with clarity, consistency, and soul-aligned strength.

When you heal, you stop reacting to wounds and start responding with wisdom. You stop shrinking to avoid rejection and start standing tall in your truth.

You no longer seek permission to be yourself, you *become* the permission.

This is leadership from the inside out.

Leadership doesn't mean control.

It doesn't mean having all the answers.

It means showing up with congruence, where your words, actions, energy, and intentions are aligned.

It means holding your boundaries without force.

Owning your voice without apology.

And choosing presence over performance.

You don't need a stage or a title to lead.

You lead when you choose awareness over autopilot.

You lead when you choose truth over people-pleasing.

You lead when you model what it looks like to come home to yourself.

And in doing so, you permit others to do the same.

Because this isn't just healing.

This is the *becoming* of who you truly are. The kind of leader the world needs now.

THE JOURNEY IS ONGOING - BUT YOU'RE EQUIPPED

Healing isn't a destination. It's a lifelong unfolding. Integration doesn't mean you will never wobble again. It means that when life challenges you, *you now know how to meet yourself differently.* You've built the inner architecture to return to truth with compassion, with clarity, and without losing yourself in the noise.

Old voices may still whisper:

"You're not enough."
"They won't understand."
"Don't rock the boat."

But now you recognise them for what they are: echoes from the past, not truth from your present.

You don't need those voices to disappear.

You need to remember they no longer lead you.

What once took you days to recover from may now take minutes.

What once felt like truth is now recognisable as trauma.

And what once left you silent now calls you to speak, not perfectly, but powerfully.

Because proper integration looks like this:

- Triggers arise, but they no longer hijack your identity
- Fearful voices appear, but your Higher Self leads the response
- Emotion flows, but it no longer floods
- Boundaries are tested, but you hold them with grace
- You don't override your needs, you honour them.

You've learned how to decode your nervous system.

How to speak from the soul, not survival.

How to notice when your old programming is running and how to step back into presence gently.

This is the real gift of the work you've done:

Not perfection.
But a powerful return.
You are no longer trying to become yourself.

You're remembering that you always were.

WHAT SOUL INTEGRITY LOOKS LIKE IN REAL LIFE

In leadership:

Instead of over-promising to be liked or over-controlling to be respected, you speak with clarity. You say what you mean, with compassion and boundaries. You stop performing to be enough, and lead from a place of grounded truth.

> Example: *"Right now, I can't take that on, but let's explore a timeline that works for both of us."*

In parenting:

Instead of reacting from inherited patterns; shaming, snapping, rescuing, you pause and respond from the Adult Self. You model emotional responsibility. You apologise when you slip. You repair instead of blaming.

> Example: *"I noticed I raised my voice earlier. That's not how I want to speak to you. I'm feeling overwhelmed, and I'm working on it."*

In partnership:

Instead of silent resentment or over-explaining, you communicate directly, even when it's vulnerable. You speak what's real, not to control, but to connect.

> Example: *"When I don't hear back from you, my old abandonment wound gets activated. I know it's not your job to fix that, but I want to be honest and work through it with you, not against you."*

In personal life:

You stop abandoning yourself to avoid discomfort. You say no when you need to. You stop apologising for your truth. You check in with your Higher Self, not your fear, before making decisions.

Example: *"I'm choosing not to go to that event. I know people might not understand, but I'm honouring what I need."*

Living Soul Integrity Means:

- Choosing **congruence over performance**, even when others don't approve
- Letting the **Higher Self guide your communication**, not your wounded parts
- Making the **unconscious conscious**, again and again, because growth is not a destination, but a devotion.

FINAL ALIGNMENT PRACTICE: YOUR SOUL-LED CONTRACT

There comes a moment on every inner journey where insight becomes embodiment, where knowledge is no longer just something you understand, but something you *live*.

You've come home to your voice. You've uncovered the architecture of your inner world, your Inner Child, your Inner Parent, your Adult Self, your Higher Self. You've begun to rewire the patterns that once kept you silent, small, reactive, or over-functioning.

But this work doesn't end with awareness.

It deepens through **intention**.

It integrates through **choice**.

This final reflection is your opportunity to anchor that choice, to write a *conscious contract* with your soul. Not a promise of perfection. But a personal declaration of what you now choose to embody in your life, your voice, and your leadership.

Soul-Led Contract: "I Commit To..."

Take a moment. Ground yourself. Breathe deeply. And write, in your own words, a declaration of how you will honour your growth.

You may start with the phrase:

"I commit to…"

And complete it with your sacred intentions, or use and expand on the ones below:

- **Listening to my system** and no longer overriding it in the name of productivity, people-pleasing, or perfection
- **Pausing before I react** allowing presence, not programming, to guide my response
- **Speaking my truth with compassion** even when it's uncomfortable, even when it shakes
- **Letting my Higher Self lead my voice** with clarity, calmness, and courage
- **Setting boundaries that honour my soul**, not to push others away, but to stay close to my integrity
- **Choosing growth over avoidance** even when the old patterns feel familiar
- **Returning to myself, again and again** because healing is not about never falling, but about how lovingly you rise.

Why This Matters

When you write your soul-led contract, you move from insight into embodiment. You're no longer just a reader, you become an active participant in your own becoming. You align your voice with your values, and in doing so, you send a powerful message to your body, your soul, your system: *I'm ready to live the shift.*

This isn't the end of your journey.

It's the beginning of speaking and living your truth out loud, on purpose, and in complete alignment with who you are.

REFLECTION & INTEGRATION

Reflection Prompt - Integration Awareness

Ask yourself:

- *"What's different in me now that can't be unseen?"*

Let this answer rise from within, not as a list, but as a knowing.

- What inner voice have I learned to hear more clearly? My Inner Child, Inner Parent, Adult Self, or Higher Self?
- In what ways do I now lead myself differently than before?
- Where am I no longer led by fear, but guided by truth?

Alignment Practice - Return to Presence

Today, pause during a moment of tension or decision-making and gently ask:

- Which part of me is speaking right now?
- What would my Higher Self choose in this moment?
- How can I honour both my humanity and my soul in how I respond?

Journal Reflection - Soul Integrity in Daily Life

Write freely on the following:

- Where in my life am I now choosing congruence over performance?
- When did I last feel proud of honouring my truth, even if it was hard?
- What am I no longer willing to sacrifice for approval or safety?

Final Realignment Prompt

Take a breath. Place your hand over your heart and ask:

- What does it mean for me to live the shift, not just understand it?
- What commitment do I now make, to my voice, my truth, and my soul-led path?

Remember the four "D's" before reacting:	
Delay	so you can bring your awareness into your Adult Self
Decode	what your Inner Child and Inner Parent are asking for
Decide	on the best path forward with advice from your Higher Self
Deliver	the new direction forward including setting boundaries where needed

16

YOUR PATH FORWARD FROM HERE

HELPING TO HEAL OTHERS

As souls having a human experience, our purpose is to return to love, lead with compassion, and live in alignment with our truth. Once you realign with your own essence, beyond conditioning, wounds, and patterns, you begin to see clearly just how many others are still living in disconnection from their own.

But here's the truth: you cannot awaken someone who isn't ready to meet themselves.

Inner transformation is a sacred, self-initiated journey of personal growth. You cannot force it. And yet, one of the most potent catalysts for others is witnessing someone else living their truth. Your embodiment becomes a mirror. Your healing becomes an invitation.

When others are still caught in unconscious patterns, reacting from pain, living from protection, unable to fully access their mind, body, and soul, you may feel a deep desire to help. But healing can't be imposed. They must feel the call from within. They must be willing to witness their pain and choose to break the cycle. Until then, your role is not to fix, but to model, to hold space, and to love without attachment.

You may be their lighthouse, not their rescue boat.

That means: No blame. No judgment. No urgency.

Many people only awaken after a breakdown, a moment when their inner structure collapses. The Inner Parent, once rigid and controlling, realises it cannot hold the system together anymore. The image it had of a "perfect" life, free of pain, grief, or failure, shatters. And in the wake of that collapse, something sacred stirs: the voice of the soul begins to rise.

This is the initiation of resurrection.

In this space, the Inner Parent is no longer in control. It may be in shock, desperately seeking sympathy, grieving its loss of control, and in negativity victimhood. But this collapse is not failure. It's the beginning of truth. It's often in these moments that the Higher Self steps in most clearly.

You've likely experienced this yourself, after the loss of a job or health, a relationship, a loved one, or a role you built your identity around. What felt like devastation was also the doorway to your realignment. The part of you that once led from survival surrendered, and a new Self emerged.

So, when you see someone stuck in suffering, meet them with compassion, but don't enable their stagnation. Don't hold them there without direction. Yes, let them feel their pain. This is necessary, as in suffering, the resurrection can begin. Gently begin to ask the reflective questions that nudge the soul forward:

- What do you feel you need most right now?
- What small step could help you shift, even slightly?

- If your Higher Self were guiding you, what might it say?

If they don't know, offer possibilities, but ask *them* to make a choice. Choice empowers. Action, even a small one, loosens the grip of paralysis and begins the process of resurrection.

Because the truth is: until the Inner Parent surrenders, the Higher Self cannot fully lead.

This is not a mistake in the human journey. It's an essential rite of passage.

The breakdown of control is often what creates space for true transformation.

So, hold others with softness, not saviourhood as much as you want their pain to stop.

Observe their suffering without attaching to their outcomes.

Guide with presence, not pressure.

And remember, every soul awakens on its own timeline.

This is what it means to lead with love and soul integrity. To guide without control. To support without rescuing. To be a mirror of possibility, not a measure of success.

This is how we create healing spaces. Where others feel safe enough to meet themselves.

And this is how we honour the deepest truth of this human experience:

That each of us is here to return home to ourselves, at our own pace, with the right support, and through the wisdom of our unfolding.

My deepest hope is that, even if you can't process it all at once, even if the changes feel slow or the path uncertain, you'll permit yourself to evolve at your own pace. May you allow space for integration, compassion for your humanness, and trust in your timing.

You came here for more than survival. You came to remember.

> To live with clarity.
> To love with integrity.
> To lead with soul.
> You are here not by accident, but with purpose.

This life, this body, this voice, is the sacred classroom where your soul chose to grow.

Welcome home.

NEXT STEPS...

You can download your workbook for all the *Reflections & Integrations* mentioned in this book, visit ⇨ **lizatherton.com/rkm-workbook**

Ready to Go Deeper?

For over 25 years, I've helped thousands of people learn to hear their Higher Self's voice, reclaim it and realign with their soul's purpose, combining grounded spiritual tools, subconscious change work, and the *PsycheIQ™ Alignment Method* I've developed through decades of client work. Now, with neuroscience-based techniques added to the process, that transformation is not only deeper, it's faster.

When you're ready to go beyond insight, and truly clear the patterns at the root that keep you stuck, that's where the **Rewrite & Ignite™**

Coaching Program begins.

And unlike traditional mindset tools or talk therapy, **Rewrite & Ignite**™ works at the level of the nervous system, the subconscious mind, and the soul, where real, lasting change begins.

Rewrite & Ignite™ Program is a 6-week neuroscience-based program designed for purpose-driven individuals, leaders, and entrepreneurs and who are ready to eliminate mental and emotional blocks, strengthen their confidence, and create meaningful success from a place of truth and alignment.

If this book has helped you reconnect with your Higher Self, understand your triggers, and reclaim your voice, **Rewrite & Ignite**™ will help you embody it. It's not just about growth. It's about realignment. It's about transformation that lasts.

This is the advanced work: where subconscious blocks are released, emotional layers are cleared, and your authentic voice and purpose are restored. Inside the program, you'll:

- Release subconscious survival patterns that have been silently running your life
- Dissolve emotional blocks that traditional talk therapy often can't reach
- Rewire your brain and body using the most powerful tools from neuroscience, somatic integration, and soul-aligned coaching
- Learn how to lead, love, and live from your integrated self, not your conditioned past

If you're ready to stop performing… and start leading from the inside out, I invite you to begin your life's next chapter inside **Rewrite & Ignite**™.

Visit ⇨ **rewriteandignite.com** to learn more.

NEXT STEPS

www.ingramcontent.com/pod-product-compliance
Lightning Source LLC
Chambersburg PA
CBHW062033290426
44109CB00026B/2617